Sales Force Compensation: Trends and Research Opportunities

Other titles in Foundations and Trends® in Marketing

Entertainment Marketing
Natasha Zhang Foutz
ISBN: 978-1-68083-332-4

The Cultural Meaning of Brands
Carlos J. Torelli, Maria A. Rodas and Jennifer L. Stoner
ISBN: 978-1-68083-286-0

Ethnography for Marketing and Consumer Research
Alladi Venkatesh, David Crockett, Samantha Cross and Steven Chen
ISBN: 978-1-68083-234-1

The Information-Economics Perspective on Brand Equity
Tulin Erdem and Joffre Swait
ISBN: 978-1-68083-168-9

Sales Force Compensation: Trends and Research Opportunities

Dominique Rouziès
HEC Paris, France
rouzies@hec.fr

Vincent Onyemah
Babson College, USA
vonyemah@babson.edu

Boston — Delft

Foundations and Trends® in Marketing

Published, sold and distributed by:
now Publishers Inc.
PO Box 1024
Hanover, MA 02339
United States
Tel. +1-781-985-4510
www.nowpublishers.com
sales@nowpublishers.com

Outside North America:
now Publishers Inc.
PO Box 179
2600 AD Delft
The Netherlands
Tel. +31-6-51115274

The preferred citation for this publication is

R. Rouziès and V. Onyemah. *Sales Force Compensation: Trends and Research Opportunities.* Foundations and Trends® in Marketing, vol. 11, no. 3, pp. 143–214, 2018.

ISBN: 978-1-68083-488-8
© 2018 R. Rouziès and V. Onyemah

Foundations and Trends® in Marketing
Volume 11, Issue 3, 2018
Editorial Board

Editorial Scope

Topics

Foundations and Trends® in Marketing publishes survey and tutorial articles in the following topics:

- B2B Marketing
- Bayesian Models
- Behavioral Decision Making
- Branding and Brand Equity
- Channel Management
- Choice Modeling
- Comparative Market Structure
- Competitive Marketing Strategy
- Conjoint Analysis
- Customer Equity
- Customer Relationship Management
- Game Theoretic Models
- Group Choice and Negotiation
- Discrete Choice Models
- Individual Decision Making

- Marketing Decisions Models
- Market Forecasting
- Marketing Information Systems
- Market Response Models
- Market Segmentation
- Market Share Analysis
- Multi-channel Marketing
- New Product Diffusion
- Pricing Models
- Product Development
- Product Innovation
- Sales Forecasting
- Sales Force Management
- Sales Promotion
- Services Marketing
- Stochastic Model

Information for Librarians

Foundations and Trends® in Marketing, 2018, Volume 11, 4 issues. ISSN paper version 1555-0753. ISSN online version 1555-0761. Also available as a combined paper and online subscription.

Contents

Sales Force Compensation: Trends and Research Opportunities

Dominique Rouziès[1] and Vincent Onyemah[2]

[1]*HEC Paris, France; rouzies@hec.fr*
[2]*Babson College, USA; vonyemah@babson.edu*

ABSTRACT

Altogether, when designing sales force compensation, decision makers are faced with a complex issue involving many
variables, some of which are unobservable, interdependent,
or uncertain. Moreover, compensation is often viewed as
salespeople's primary motivator and in many corporations,
it is the dominant sales expense. The objective of this monograph is to review the many insights provided by empirical
research to date, some of which are just emerging in the
marketing literature. We first discuss how plans should be
designed according to the dominant research stream and
contrast research findings with actual sales force compensation policies. Then, we highlight topics related to sales
force compensation that are notably under-researched and
show how taking them into account will enrich knowledge
on compensation. Finally, we conclude with future trends
in sales force compensation.

© Dominique Rouziès and Vincent Onyemah (2018), "Sales Force Compensation:
Trends and Research Opportunities", Foundations and Trends® in Marketing: Vol. 11,
No. 3, pp 143–214. DOI: 10.1561/1700000046.

1

Introduction

Few professions have their compensation as scrutinized as business-to-business (B2B) salespeople. Salespeople's compensation, like that for CEOs, has triggered many debates. Experts have examined issues ranging from compensation levels, structures, caps, complexity, fairness, gaps with other members of the organization, to menus of compensation. But unlike CEOs who are usually recognized as crucial members of organizations, salespeople's critical role is rarely acknowledged. A recent article in *The Economist* labels salespeople as the "unsung heroes of business" (2011). Indeed, salespeople are seldom portrayed as important to organizational success. However, without their contribution, there would not be revenues because customers would not be served, contracts would not be signed and sales would not be created. In fact, without their work, there would not be strong relationships with customers, let alone lasting ones. Indeed, "selling is the horse that pulls the cart of business" (Delves Broughton, 2012). In fact, sales represent a much bigger portion of a firm's employees than any other function (Delves Broughton, 2012). Thus, about one in nine or ten employees work in sales in Europe and North America respectively (Eurostat, 2009; U.S. Bureau of Labor Statistics, 2015).

Despite its economic and corporate importance though, surprisingly, sales has traditionally carried a stigma on both academic and industry fronts: academics have viewed sales research as lacking both theoretical foundations and marketing relevance while industry experts have failed to see its applicability (Ahearne, 2017). More pressing is the concern that sales careers spark so limited interest nowadays that firms have a hard time recruiting salespeople (Weber, 2015). In many sectors, however, sales jobs have little to do with the "car sales job" stereotype. Numerous experts describe the analytical and creative dimensions of current sales jobs (e.g., Adamson *et al.*, 2013). They point to the necessity for salespeople to use more strategic approaches because customers have now access to more information, have become more knowledgeable about available solutions to their problem and generally estimate the price they are willing to pay before they meet a salesperson. All in all, sales jobs tend to involve different and rarer skills than before. So why is salespeople's image still so poor? This may be because it allows many other employees to complain about the unfairness of their special treatment (e.g., Goltz, 2013). Indeed, sales jobs have idiosyncrasies (Gomez-Mejia and Balkin, 1992) that may justify special treatment in organizations. No other employee is in direct contact and in charge of a firm's most precious asset: its customers' relationships (Zoltners *et al.*, 2009, p. 3). For this reason, salespeople's success is critical to their organizations' performance. This success however, may not be easy to achieve for at least three major reasons. First, because salespeople need to serve their customers' best interests as much as their organizations, they may experience role conflict. Second, often times salespeople experience role ambiguity: they often work far from their supervisors, they are likely to possess knowledge about customers that their supervisors do not have. Moreover, they can use selling strategies that supervisors cannot observe. It is difficult for supervisors in these conditions to clarify their sales role or to reward their salespeople accordingly. Third, because environmental conditions evolve and firms regularly market new offers, sales leaders need to fine-tune their salespeople's compensation plans. However, they are frequently complex, and the fine tuning implies that the sales goals are a moving target. Such issues can prevent salespeople from concentrating their selling efforts on activities that are in the best interest of their firm.

Altogether, when designing sales force compensation, decision makers are faced with a complex issue involving many variables, some of which are unobservable, interdependent, or uncertain. Moreover, compensation is often viewed as salespeople's primary motivator and in many corporations, it is the dominant sales expense. The objective of this monograph is to review the many insights provided by empirical research to date, some of which are just emerging in the marketing literature. We first discuss how plans should be designed according to the dominant research stream and contrast research findings with actual sales force compensation policies. Then, we highlight topics related to sales force compensation that are notably under-researched and show how taking them into account will enrich knowledge on compensation. Finally, we conclude with future trends in sales force compensation.

2

Previous Research[1]

The myriad of compensation plans used in companies (see Tables 1 and 2) provides evidence of sales managers' task difficulty- selecting the best plan. Indeed, compensation plans typically vary along two dimensions of (1) fixed/variable and (2) conditional/non-conditional upon a predetermined performance level, yielding four categories of compensation schemes. First, compensation plans may feature fixed and non-conditional components, e.g., salary, fringe benefits, and travel or car expense allowances. A second class of remuneration components consists of incentive payments that includes bonuses. Bonuses are fixed elements, conditional upon a predetermined performance level. They usually take into account other factors in addition to sales volume (e.g., new account acquisition, account retention, territory coverage, managerial appraisal, expense savings, profit on sales, sales contests, number of calls, etc.). Typically, bonuses are functions of individual sales over some quota, or group sales volume. Fixed rate commissions and various allocations for expenses are elements of the third class of variable and non-conditional remuneration components. This class of incentive payments is usually closely related to sales volume (value

---

[1]This section is an adapted extract from Rouziès (1992).

Table 1: International survey of salespeople's compensation* (adapted from Korn & Ferry – Hay group, 2017)

	Base Salary			% Variable Pay			Total Cash		
	Quarter 3	Median	Quarter 1	Quarter 3	Median	Quarter 1	Quarter 3	Median	Quarter 1
France (€)									
Consumer Goods	40 302	35 382	30 513	9	5	2	50 315	42 384	35 547
Financial Services	39 601	35 642	32 360	29	11	3	48 893	43 243	37 849
High Technology	41 522	35 645	31 499	16	7	3	48 118	40 627	36 562
Industrial Goods	40 766	35 347	30 656	10	5	2	45 315	39 394	34 397
Other Industries	45 407	41 008	36 603	9	6	3	53 981	45 983	41 191
Professional Services	40 085	28 593	26 796	15	9	4	43 249	32 631	30 051
Germany (€)									
Consumer Goods	61 471	52 095	43 627	12	6	3	66 595	55 736	47 058
Financial Services		na			na			na	
High Technology	58 914	50 747	46 162	17	6	4	64 259	53 388	49 915
Industrial Goods	58 205	49 779	43 289	10	5	3	61 404	52 857	45 746
Other Industries	64 495	58 372	51 786	10	7	3	69 546	60 865	53 085
Professional Services		43 154		na				43 628	
Italy (€)									
Consumer Goods	42 360	36 727	30 450	19	9	4	47 277	40 501	34 598
Financial Services		38 734			–			39 046	
High Technology		35 725			7			39 461	
Industrial Goods	42 348	34 431	30 969	22	12	7	48 712	37 561	33 904
Other Industries	42 570	36 392	35 625	7	4	–	44 116	37 215	36 121
Professional Services		na			na			na	

Table 1: Continued

	Base Salary			% Variable Pay			Total Cash		
	Quarter 3	Median	Quarter 1	Quarter 3	Median	Quarter 1	Quarter 3	Median	Quarter 1
Netherlands (€)									
Consumer Goods	50 231	44 364	38 768	9	5	2	53 750	46 873	39 719
Financial Services	52 424	48 727	43 705	9	5	3	54 298	50 032	45 842
High Technology	50 860	45 510	40 707	16	9	5	55 955	48 554	42 000
Industrial Goods	49 553	43 193	38 405	9	5	2	51 135	44 714	39 812
Other Industries	53 992	48 642	42 534	8	3	2	57 185	50 549	43 769
Professional Services	46 822	40 843	35 546	9	4	0	49 214	42 630	36 783
United Kingdom (£)									
Consumer Goods	34 624	30 187	26 797	10	6	3	36 988	31 761	27 765
Financial Services	31 138	28 070	25 266	8	6	4	35 546	29 962	27 561
High Technology	34 420	29 794	25 731	17	6	4	36 437	32 663	27 944
Industrial Goods	32 341	29 170	25 464	12	7	5	35 275	30 873	27 941
Other Industries	34 424	30 196	26 495	10	5	1	36 364	31 824	28 094
Professional Services	34 867	27 654	25 136	7	4	–	41 629	29 384	28 168
USA ($)									
Consumer Goods	58 279	49 136	42 148	18	7	1	66 898	53 650	44 931
Financial Services	59 498	52 635	46 560	27	10	3	75 086	60 001	51 184
High Technology		na			na			na	
Industrial Goods	65 100	59 376	53 343	10	4	1	68 986	60 922	54 609
Other Industries	75 818	66 430	58 151	18	7	3	85 562	71 912	63 232
Professional Services		na			na			na	

Note: Figures corresponding to 200–320 Hay points and Hay levels 12, 13 and 14.

Table 2: International survey of sales managers' compensation (adapted from Korn & Ferry – Hay group, 2017)

	Base Salary			% Variable Pay			Total Cash		
	Quarter 3	Median	Quarter 1	Quarter 3	Median	Quarter 1	Quarter 3	Median	Quarter 1
France (€)									
Consumer Goods	101 066	89 582	78 617	19	14	10	128 644	112 655	95 360
Financial Services	104 863	90 105	80 848	24	16	10	128 612	116 702	94 222
High Technology	100 598	89 494	79 873	21	12	8	122 159	107 680	94 770
Industrial Goods	101 556	88 491	77 031	19	11	5	119 820	103 171	87 893
Other Industries	113 377	101 036	91 092	20	14	9	138 903	119 314	105 046
Professional Services	99 650	84 788	73 633	29	23	14	107 332	102 724	80 857
Germany (€)									
Consumer Goods	135 528	118 305	105 088	26	18	11	163 991	138 323	115 028
Financial Services		109 600		28				117 400	
High Technology	126 337	111 818	97 025	27	17	14	150 357	131 549	110 650
Industrial Goods	121 081	109 415	99 430	20	13	7	139 286	123 177	111 813
Other Industries	134 624	122 460	109 394	24	18	11	158 113	142 800	124 733
Professional Services		107 389		9				109 725	
Italy (€)									
Consumer Goods	112 040	97 016	85 431	26	20	11	139 816	115 544	97 619
Financial Services	118 952	99 544	84 435	15	8	1	128 042	107 156	90 217
High Technology	105 269	90 442	74 205	24	12	3	116 867	101 412	82 604
Industrial Goods	109 006	93 166	77 972	25	16	10	130 532	109 703	88 429
Other Industries	113 420	98 577	81 449	20	13	4	131 265	109 318	88 160
Professional Services		na		na				na	

Table 2: Continued

	Base Salary			% Variable Pay			Total Cash		
	Quarter 3	Median	Quarter 1	Quarter 3	Median	Quarter 1	Quarter 3	Median	Quarter 1
Netherlands (€)									
Consumer Goods	114 868	106 865	97 386	18	13	7	132 544	116 556	107 195
Financial Services	127 431	118 618	107 598	19	14	4	149 148	127 117	114 172
High Technology	111 421	102 680	92 879	12	6	1	117 017	103 798	94 092
Industrial Goods	113 014	101 738	89 221	18	8	4	122 831	109 434	94 633
Other Industries	125 548	115 013	104 455	20	13	8	142 136	128 442	113 875
Professional Services	99 934	91 103	84 556	9	4	1	105 633	95 922	86 640
United Kingdom (£)									
Consumer Goods	86 750	77 076	69 259	21	14	8	102 969	89 424	78 583
Financial Services	96 691	86 750	75 563	34	18	9	122 528	103 667	84 362
High Technology	86 647	74 935	66 475	16	10	5	93 742	82 641	71 300
Industrial Goods	85 541	74 710	66 377	18	12	5	97 175	80 918	72 398
Other Industries	92 012	81 503	71 448	21	14	7	106 632	91 716	79 736
Professional Services	97 460	85 050	73 231	27	18	8	122 888	99 084	84 958
USA ($)									
Consumer Goods	165 273	145 896	127 164	31	21	9	208 479	173 776	147 158
Financial Services	157 083	132 050	117 873	46	23	11	212 248	168 747	139 937
High Technology	178 888	147 065	135 998	23	15	7	207 001	163 689	149 202
Industrial Goods	154 685	138 877	121 044	24	12	4	183 234	152 691	130 872
Other Industries	168 399	153 360	137 182	25	18	10	207 204	179 837	156 638
Professional Services		na			na			na	

Note: Figures corresponding to 550–850 Hay points and Hay levels 18, 19 and 20.

or unit). In addition, fixed commission rates may differ according to the type of product line sold by the salesperson. Finally, the fourth class of remuneration components (variable and conditional) includes progressive (regressive) rate commissions, the rates of which increase (decrease) with increasing sales (Coughlan and Sen, 1989). The possible combinations of these remuneration components present various strengths and weaknesses that numerous scholars studied as we explain shortly.

The bulk of empirical sales force compensation research can be divided into four different areas: (1) the traditional sales management literature, which is descriptive and based on experiential work or statements of opinions, (2) expectancy motivation studies, (3) analytical models of optimal forms of sales force compensation plans, and (4) integrated models typically focusing on the control function of sales force compensation plans. The remainder of this chapter reviews the sales force compensation literature along these four streams of research.

2.1   The Traditional Sales Management Literature

Much of the traditional sales force management literature on compensation is either experiential or inherited from conjectures based on observations. One notable exception includes Darmon (1974). The major merits and demerits of three basic compensation plans: salary, commission, and combination plans have long been identified in this traditional sales management literature (e.g., Day and Bennett, 1962).

Straight salary plans. Salespeople receive pay at a fixed rate, although salaries may be adjusted in the long run to reflect productivity. Several principles are known about this kind of compensation. First, the income regularity and stability of salary plans are likely to have a positive impact on salespeople's job satisfaction and to reduce turnover rate. Second, the control of sales managers over salespeople's activities is enhanced through the loyalty that is likely to result from job satisfaction. Moreover, straight salary plans are deemed appropriate when it is difficult to assess salespeople's inputs into the selling task. But such a measurement problem results in highly subjective performance evaluation, since the sales personnel will be evaluated on perceived behaviors rather than on objective indicators (e.g., sales). Third, salary plans provide favorable grounds to motivate salespeople to work consistently with the firm's strategy. Finally, when a new strategy requires different allocation of resources to territories, product lines, or customers, salary plans provide a high degree of flexibility for such changes. In that case, the firm bears the risk of uncertainty linked to prospecting new territories, selling new product lines, contacting new customers. Moreover, salary plans lead to greater profits under favorable economic conditions because selling costs are fixed.

Commission plans provide salespeople with compensations in direct proportion to their productivity. Therefore, salespeople are poorly motivated and frustrated when factors beyond their control exert a strong influence on their productivity. For exemple, if a new competitor moves in their territory, they may experience difficulties to sell their products/services. In such a case, the turnover rate tends to increase dramatically. However, when sales results are not volatile, commission plans provide the firm with a powerful motivational tool. Part of this motivation is related to the immediate feedback of achievement that commission schemes provide. In addition, under commission plans salespeople enjoy a nearly total freedom of operation. In terms of strategy, commission plans offer major advantages when a firm's financial position is weak, because the company's investment risk is minimized.

Combination systems are the most common salesforce compensation plans. Specifically, in addition to a salary, combined plans use some type of incentive pay (e.g., commission, bonus). In general, their purpose is to leverage the strength of the two methods, while overcoming their weaknesses. Therefore, depending on their structure, an analysis of their merits and demerits is similar to the analysis of salary and commission plans just stated. In the development of a compensation plan, a critical issue is the emphasis placed on salary versus incentive compensation. Three major factors influence the structure of combination plans according to this body of literature: job dimensions, environment, and business strategy. When the salesperson's skills and primary function are important dimensions, a higher amount of incentive is advocated. For instance, when personal skills are important in making sales, or when the primary function is to sell new accounts, lower amounts of salary are recommended. When it is difficult to measure the sales impact of sales-people because of the selling method used (technical or team selling), or the importance of other parts of the marketing program (high advertise-ment, sales promotion, significant competitive advantage of product), then decreased amounts of incentive compensation are advocated.

Finally, the combination plan structure should account for a lower proportion of incentive to total pay when environmental factors exert a strong influence on selling activities. In that latter case, the company bears the risk linked to environmental uncertainty.

This brief review shows how the sales management literature reflects the "conventional wisdom" about the design of effective compensation systems (Walker *et al.*, 1977). Furthermore, inconsistencies can be readily identified in this literature. For example, John and Weitz (1989), note that the recommended use of more salary for complex selling tasks (technical sales for example) contradicts the prescription to increase the level of incentive pay when the salesperson's skills (technical skills, for example) are determinant in making sales. Note that Rouziès *et al.* (2009) report that higher levels of job challenge do not necessitate, or nearly compensate, for lower levels of financial incentives. All in all, more research is needed to test the insights provided by the traditional sales management literature.

2.2   The Expectancy Motivation Literature

Several decades ago, Walker *et al.* (1977) introduced a behavioral model of salesperson's performance (modified in Churchill *et al.*, 1985) which prompted considerable research. They developed several propositions about the characteristics of salespeople and their work environment that help explain salespeople's performance. Drawing on Vroom's expectancy theory (1964), they argued that sales personnel's performance is a multiplicative function of motivation, aptitude, skill levels and role perceptions. They defined the motivation component of their model as being determined by three sets of perceptions: valences for rewards, expectancies, and instrumentalities.

In the context of compensation, this stream of research has produced several interesting results. Perhaps the best known finding is that compensation brings the highest level of salespeople's motivation. Other empirical findings include, among others, the negative relationships existing between the salespersons' pay level and pay valence (or their desire to obtain additional amounts of pay); or between the salespersons' satisfaction with pay and pay valence.

Although this stream of research produced some interesting results, as with most research, this body of research does have some limitations. One of its most important limitations is the lack of operational guidance offered to sales managers. Indeed, it would be interesting to investigate the type of compensation schemes leading to the best outcomes for both the sales force and the firm. Research based on microeconomics, presented shortly, tries to answer that call.

2.3 Models of Optimal Sales Force Compensation

To date, analytical and theoretical work on sales force compensation has been dominated by agency theory, which focuses on trying to optimize compensation plans (in total pay and in the ratio of salary to variable pay). In this framework, firms and salespeople have diverging goals and risk preferences, and salespeople's behaviors are not observable (so that they may be shirking). In other words, studies investigate the risk-adjusted expected compensation level of a salesperson whose next-best earning opportunity should be less attractive, in the best interest of the firm. This stream of research has generated predictions about the effect of a number of variables (e.g., opportunity cost of time, size of the firm, environment uncertainty, and sales effort productivity) on optimal compensation. For a recent and extensive review, see Coughlan and Joseph (2014). In this chapter, only empirical sales force compensation studies will be featured.

2.3.1 Representative Insights

Key analytic contributions, based on agency theoretic models, rely on a number of assumptions that may be restrictive and make empirical verification difficult. First, typical agency theoretic studies focus on *a salesperson's* compensation (*not a salesforce*). In addition, they assume that salespeople are independent from one another, that they do not sell in team or even make salary comparisons. The models generally assume that salespeople are risk averse. Other assumptions include: constant marginal (non-selling) costs, asymmetry of information, identical reservation prices across salespeople, static model, or no interactions among the products in a company's portfolio.

Nevertheless, this stream of research sheds light on salesforce compensation optimal structures and levels. Most empirical studies testing agency theoretic predictions (e.g., Coughlan and Narasimhan, 1992; Joseph and Kalwani, 1995; Misra *et al.*, 2005; Rouziès *et al.*, 2009) deal with two compensation elements, fixed salary and incentive pay.

Perhaps, the most well-known prediction is the negative effect of uncertainty in the sales response function on total pay. That is, one would expect that total pay is lower for high levels of uncertainty in the sales response function. However, the empirical test of this prediction failed. Other predictions which have been empirically supported include the positive relationship between (1) a salesperson's outside earning opportunity, or (2) the effectiveness of selling effort, on the expected total income; the positive effect of (3) uncertainty in the sales response function, or (4) a salesperson's outside earning opportunity, on the optimal ratio of salary and expected total income; the negative relationship between (5) the effectiveness of selling effort, on the optimal ratio of salary and expected total income.

Besides research on compensation featuring a fixed salary and generic incentives, scholars have provided important insights on quota-bonus plans (e.g., Chung *et al.*, 2014; Steenburgh, 2008). In general, they show that bonuses help increase productivity. More specifically, they find that quarterly bonuses can be used to keep salespeople on track to achieve annual sales goals, while annual bonuses reward high performance (Coughlan and Joseph, 2014). We will review these studies in Part III as they use new methodological approaches.

2.4   Integrated Models of Compensation Practices

The fourth major stream of literature to consider emerged in the 1980s and 1990s (e.g., Anderson, 1985; Anderson and Oliver, 1987; Coughlan and Narasimhan, 1992; Eisenhardt, 1985, 1988; John and Weitz, 1989).

The conceptual models proposed in this literature typically attempt to describe the process used by sales managers to choose salary versus commission compensation. These research studies often integrate theories such as agency theory, transaction cost analysis, organizational theory, institutional theory and traditional sales management. As agency theory has been presented earlier, we will proceed with a short description of other theories integrated in those frameworks.

Transaction Cost Analysis. Adapted to the sales force compensation context, transaction cost analysis highlights the control function of compensation structures (John and Weitz, 1989). This framework suggests that the control of salespeople activities can be achieved within a firm through the control of behaviors (e.g., plans emphasizing salary), or through market like control mechanisms (e.g., outcome control through plans emphasizing incentives).

Transaction cost analysis considers market contracting as being the most efficient option because of the potential limitations of the bureaucratic system (e.g., communication distortion, uninformed decision making, inertia, etc.), and the benefits of competition (e.g., competitive pressures determine the elimination or the survival of salespeople activities) (Anderson and Oliver, 1987). Anderson (1985) and John and Weitz (1989) have applied transaction cost analysis to the choice between using direct salespeople or manufacturers' representatives.

Organization Theory. Organization theory recognizes alternative approaches to control issues (Eisenhardt, 1985). The first approach deals with performance evaluation, that is monitoring and rewarding salespeople. The second approach to the control of salespeople activities addresses the issue of socialization of salespeople that would ultimately lead to preference congruence between the firm and the salesperson. Organization theory considers that the choice between these strategies depends on varying degrees of outcome measurability and task programmability (e.g., knowledge by the sales managers of the behaviors required to achieve desired results) (Eisenhardt, 1985). As will be shown later, organization theory can provide researchers with a powerful tool for predicting compensation practices.

Institutional Theory. The core concept of institutional theory is that conformity to norms shapes organization mechanisms. In other words, the basic rule governing organizations is legitimacy (Eisenhardt, 1988).

Therefore, sales force compensation studies drawing on this theoretical framework (1) advocate the investigation of industry and company norms and traditions and (2) validate this model (Eisenhardt, 1988). All in all, the key insights derived from this conceptual modeling of compensation practices fall into four major categories: (1) evaluation issues, (2) environmental -, (3) selling task -, or (4) organization-characteristics as explained next.

2.4.1 Evaluation Issues

The measurability of salespeople performance appears to be a strong determinant of the use of salary (Anderson, 1985; John and Weitz, 1989). In short, the more difficult the performance assessment, the more likely the use of salaries (over variable compensation components). The performance evaluation issue is a construct critical to the choice of compensation plan as proposed by three schools of thought: agency theory, transaction cost analysis, and traditional sales management. About half of the propositions derived by these schools of thought deal with the cost of outcome measurement (Eisenhardt, 1985) and the difficulty of assessing performance through outcome measurement (Anderson, 1985; John and Weitz, 1989). In other words, when output measures (e.g, value or volume sales, number of new customers, profits, etc.) do not enable firms to assess salespeople performance, firms rely more heavily on input (i.e., behavioral and process) measures. The remaining proposition provides evidence for the negative relationship existing between the difficulty of input measurement and the likelihood of using salary (John and Weitz, 1989). In a similar vein, Eisenhardt (1985) stresses the likelihood of fixed compensation when performance assessment is achieved through behavior measurement.

In summary, although the empirical findings related to the issue of performance evaluation appear to be very consistent, further investigation of what has been called "internal uncertainty", namely, the lack of knowledge about the activities in which salespeople should engage to achieve a given level of performance (Anderson, 1985), would still be welcome.

2.4.2 Environmental Characteristics

Besides such issues of "internal uncertainty", researchers have also examined empirically the issue of "external uncertainty". Spanning the three research schools of agency theory, transaction cost analysis, and traditional sales management, this construct has been explored from various angles. Nevertheless, the construct has relatively low explanatory power which generally improves when combined with low task programmability (Eisenhardt, 1988), transaction specific assets (e.g., valuable knowledge with the company) (Anderson, 1985), or more specifically, the perceived non-competitiveness of labor markets (e.g., replaceability) (John and Weitz, 1989). In other words, managers do not seem to cope with increasing uncertainty through changes in compensation practices, unless they can no longer effectively monitor salesperson performance, or unless the collective experience of their salesforce is too valuable for the firm to risk losing.

Another environmental characteristic has been rightfully pointed out by Coughlan and Narasimhan (1992). They have provided evidence of the significant effect of opportunity costs on the likelihood of using salary.

These findings point out an additional implication. The agency theory concept of salesforce to firm risk transfer (under conditions of environmental uncertainty) through the use of fixed compensation plans seems to account for a very modest share of control decisions. Moreover, it may be useful to distinguish between the various forms of uncertainty as suggested by Anderson and Oliver (1987) and John and Weitz (1989).

2.4.3 Selling Task Characteristics

Eisenhardt (1985, 1988) provides strong empirical support for the critical importance of task characteristics in terms of compensation practice predictions. The strongest determinant reported is the level of task programmability, that is, the knowledge of the transformation process. Sales managers' awareness of which actions lead to a desired level of performance is crucial in deciding whether commissions or salaries should be used. The performance of a person doing highly programmable tasks is easier to assess and will result in behavior control policies based on salary compensation plans. However, these conclusions should be treated with caution because of the particularity of the setting used by Eisenhardt (1985, 1988), namely being set in retailing as compared to industrial setting for the other studies.

Anderson (1985) and John and Weitz (1989) uncover strong alternative predictors related to the nature of the selling job which appear to be consistent with one another. The more time devoted purely to selling by salespeople, the more likely use of incentive compensation (John and Weitz, 1989). This finding corroborates that of Anderson (1985) regarding the positive relationship between the importance of non-selling activities and the use of fixed compensation plans. In a similar vein, the more customization of an offering by salespeople to customers, the less likely is the use of salary plans (John and Weitz, 1989). This conclusion is in keeping with Anderson's result (1985) related to customer loyalty, since it seems reasonnable to believe that customers will be more loyal if they receive tailored offerings from salespeople. Alternatively, the use of salary plans decreases as the information needs of customers increase (John and Weitz, 1989). This conclusion matches the previous finding related to the importance of non-selling activities in the job. Clearly, providing the information customers are asking for, is part of the accounts servicing. And finally, brand specific knowledge and confidential information retention go along with salary plans, that is, firms want to keep salespeople who are too valuable to lose.

2.4.4 Organizational Characteristics

Organizational characteristics have an influence on the firm's choice of a compensation plan. For example, the institutional paradigm provides a good description of retail compensation policies. Thus, older stores as well as shoe stores use commissions, and these conclusions are consistent with the retail business history (Eisenhardt, 1988).

The findings of John and Weitz (1989) and Eisenhardt (1988) regarding, respectively, the size of the salesforce and the span of control are in keeping with previous conclusions. The bigger the salesforce, the less likely the use of fixed salary. These findings reinforce the transaction cost analysis assumption pertaining to the superiority of market like control mechanisms. In other words, the bigger the salesforce, the more difficult the intrafirm control procedures, therefore, the less likely the use of salaries. In a similar vein, the extent of managerial span of control varies in inverse fashion with the choice of fixed compensation plans. Thus, bigger spans of control go along with increasing difficulty of behavior control, leading therefore to commission plans policies. Finally, Anderson (1985) shows how salespeople selling competitive product lines are usually compensated on a fixed salary basis.

3

Understudied Aspects of Sales Force Compensation

In this chapter, we turn to topics that have mostly been neglected in the salesforce compensation literature (see Table 3 and Figure 1 for a summary). Hopefully, this will trigger more interest from scholars as these issues are essential to better understand compensation decisions.

First, in spite of a great deal of insightful research, the literature on sales force compensation (mostly based on microeconomics) has developed under the assumption of salespeople's independence (Chan *et al.*, 2014b). In other words, most sales scholars assume that salespeople's behaviors are not influenced by their coworkers (e.g., Basu *et al.*, 1985; Coughlan and Sen, 1989; Misra *et al.*, 2005). It has long been known however that most salespeople's assessments and decisions are not made in a vacuum. Salespeople who are part of a sales force, meet, observe one another and exchange information. It is therefore plausible that salespeople make decisions on the basis of their assessment of their peers' rewards, behaviors and/or outputs. Sales executives have long been aware of these premises. Indeed, a large number of sales organizations advertise their top performers and bonuses, set up leader boards and sales contests; many sales executives try to promote sales-related knowledge transfer from high performers to younger recruits; and most

Table 3: Summary of empirical sales force compensation research trends and opportunities (representative studies)

	Dominant Research Perspective	Emerging Research Opportunities
Theoretical Foundations	**Primarily economic-based approaches** Based on Agency Theory or Transaction Cost Analysis for example, (e.g., Chung et al., 2014; Coughlan and Narasimhan, 1992; Daljord et al., 2016; Dustin and Belasen, 2013; John and Weitz, 1989; Joseph and Kalwani, 1995; Krafft et al., 2004; Lal and Srinivasan, 1993; Lal et al., 1994; Lo et al., 2011; Misra et al., 2005; Misra and Nair, 2011)	**Including other theoretical approaches** Testing insights from other theoretical approaches (e.g., psychology) (e.g., Chung and Narayandas, 2017; Rouziès et al., 2017; Rouziou et al., 2018a, 2018b; Obloj and Sengul, 2012)
Compensation Plan Primary Role	**Incentive role** Focused on the ramifications of the incentive role of compensation plans (e.g., Joseph and Kalwani, 1995; Coughlan and Narasimhan, 1992; Krafft et al., 2004; Lal et al., 1994; Misra et al., 2005; Misra and Nair, 2011)	**Selection role** Focused on the selection role of compensation plans (e.g., Daljord et al., 2016; Keshavarz et al., 2017; Lo et al., 2011)
Empirical Setting	**Single country** Research conducted in a single country (e.g., Chung and Narayandas, 2017; Coughlan and Narasimhan, 1992; Daljord et al., 2016; John and Weitz, 1989; Joseph and Kalwani, 1995; Keshavarz et al., 2017; Krafft et al., 2004; Lal et al., 1994; Lo et al., 2011; Misra et al., 2005; Misra and Nair, 2011, Rouziou et al., 2018)	**Multi-country environments** Better accounting for new international environments (e.g., Hohenberg and Homburg, 2016; Rouziès et al., 2017; Rouziès et al., 2009; Segalla et al., 2006)

Table 3: Continued

	Dominant Research Perspective	Emerging Research Opportunities
Selling Environment	**Independence among salespeople** (e.g., Coughlan and Sen, 1989; Daljord *et al.*, 2016; Lal and Srinivasan, 1993; Joseph and Kalwani, 1998; Joseph and Thevaranjan, 1998; Misra *et al.*, 2005)	**Interactions among salespeople** Social comparisons and peer effects (e.g., Chan *et al.*, 2014a,b; Miao *et al.*, 2017; Rouziou *et al.*, 2018b)
Methodology	**Survey / archival / proprietary data** Survey-based research studies (e.g., John and Weitz, 1989; Krafft *et al.*, 2004; Rouziès *et al.*, 2017; Segalla *et al.*, 2006) or research using large scale administrative or proprietary databases (e.g., Coughlan and Narasimhan, 1992; Keshavarz *et al.*, 2017; Misra *et al.*, 2005; Rouziès *et al.*, 2009; Rouziou *et al.*, 2018)	**Field experiments** Research studies using field experiments (e.g., Chan *et al.*, 2014a,b; Chung and Narayandas, 2017; Dustin and Belasen, 2013; Misra and Nair, 2011)
Measurement	**Aggregate data** Analysis of a typical salesperson representative of a sales force (e.g., Coughlan and Narasimhan, 1992; John and Weitz, 1989; Krafft *et al.*, 2004; Misra *et al.*, 2005)	**Micro-level data** Analyses carried at the level of an individual salesperson (e.g., Chung *et al.*, 2014; Lal *et al.*, 1994; Lo *et al.*, 2011; Keshavarz *et al.*, 2017; Rouziès *et al.*, 2009; Rouziès *et al.*, 2017; Rouziou *et al.*, 2018)

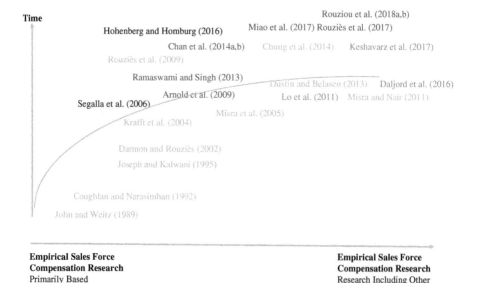

Figure 1: Summary of the empirical research on sales force compensation (representative studies).

Notes: Research primarily based on economic theories emphasizing the *Incentive role of compensation*.

Research primarily based on economic theories emphasizing the *Selection role of compensation*.

Research including other theoretical approaches and dealing with *Fairness/equity/social comparisons/peer effects*.

Research including other theoretical approaches and dealing with *Cultural mechanisms*.

firms make sure a climate of fairness exists in their sales organizations. In the next section (see 3.1), we describe how perceptions of fairness, social comparisons and peer effects matter in sales organizations.

Second, in addition to developing under the assumption of salespeople's independence, research on salesforce compensation has curiously omitted the examination of career-related issues. In other words, to the best of our knowledge, studies of salesforce compensation rarely mention how the number of years of experience of sales employees influence the way firms value sales jobs. However, recruiters generally take career history into account to assess the value of a candidate. Consequently, we will examine how firms value sales careers (see 3.2).

Furthermore, as Rouziès *et al.* (2017, p. 199) note: "research on cross-cultural sales management has not kept pace with the jobs of sales managers whose responsibilities often include the supervision of salespeople in different countries (Deloitte and Oracle, 2008)". This chapter therefore will review the influence of culture, Just World Beliefs (JWBs) and religion on sales force compensation (see 3.3).

3.1 Salespeople in their Organization

3.1.1 How Fairness Matters in Sales Force Compensation

Existing research on sales force compensation is dominated by economic theories such as transaction cost analysis (e.g., Williamson, 1981) and agency theory (e.g., Holmstrom and Milgrom, 1991). Although those approaches provide important insights as shown above, they leave other questions unanswered especially because most research in this body of literature, (1) assume salespeople are independent from one another or (2) develop optimal plans for a single salesperson. But the psychology of salespeople is equally important. In particular, since the pioneering works of Festinger (1954) and Adams (1965), the issues of social comparison and equity have triggered the interest of scholars of fairness related to pay in human resource management (e.g., Sung *et al.*, 2017), management (e.g., Fredrickson *et al.*, 2010) and economics (e.g., Falk *et al.*, 2006). Yet, the sales force compensation literature provides little evidence of the same level of interest. The neglect of fairness in the sales force compensation literature is surprising because reviews of justice research indicate that fairness in organizations matters a great deal (e.g., Colquitt *et al.*, 2001). Indeed, if employees perceive their firm or their direct supervisor are unfair, employees may decrease effort, sabotage others' efforts, behave non-cooperatively, lobby managers who assign their compensation, or leave the company: all of these reactions are detrimental to firm performance (Larkin *et al.*, 2012; Nickerson and Zenger, 2008). In fact, fairness is known to influence employees' job motivation and performance. In addition, no other profession is exposed to fairness concerns as much as sales is, because no other profession uses contests, performance publications, leader boards or performance-pay plans as widely as the sales profession does.

Next we review the sales-related literature that investigates fairness in compensation. This allows us to bring together papers focusing on various topics such as supervisory fairness, fairness as a driver of social capital or salespeople's fairness judgments referents (see Table 4 for a summary).

Supervisory Role. In one of the rare investigations of salespeople's pay-raise fairness, Ramaswami and Singh (2003) confirm the crucial role of supervisors in shaping salespeople's fairness judgments. Specifically, they investigate three fairness dimensions (interactional, distributive and procedural) widely established in the literature (Colquitt *et al.*, 2001). The *interactional* dimension of justice refers to the interpersonal treatment –including the explanations- received from employees during the enactment of the merit-pay procedures. The *procedural* dimension involves the perceived fairness of merit-pay procedures. The *distributive* dimension deals with the fairness of pay decision outcomes. In their study, Ramaswami and Singh (2003) found that the interactional dimension of justice has more effect than the procedural or the distributive ones on salespeople's job outcomes. Another interesting finding of their study is the importance of distributive fairness in influencing salespeople's job performance. All in all, their results suggest, among other things, that sales managers need to be more transparent and spend more time with salespeople in order to help them improve job performance.

Aside from focusing on specific types of fairness (i.e., procedural, distributive, interactional, interpersonal or informational justice), other research effort has examined the impact of supervisors in shaping salespeople's overall fairness judgments. Indeed, prior literature (e.g., Aryee *et al.*, 2015; Jones and Martens, 2009) suggests people's experiences of justice are better represented by perceptions of overall fairness. For example, Rouziès *et al.* (2017) show the impact of perceived management fairness on salespeople's performance pay in some environments but not in others. Their study documents the effects of overall fairness after controlling for standard economic factors (i.e., salesperson's risk diversification, firm willingness to share compensation risk, job experience and firm size). They find that salespeople's variable to total compensation

Table 4: Empirical research on equity and fairness in sales force compensation (representative studies)

	Fairness Relative to a Referent	Supervisory Fairness	Pay Fairness	Main results pertaining to compensation	Managerial implications
Ramaswami and Singh (2003)		x		Interactional justice has more effect than the procedural or the distributive ones on salespeople's job outcomes. Important role of distributive fairness in influencing salespeople's job performance.	Sales managers should put into place a performance improvement plan for salespeople. They need to be more transparent and spend more time with salespeople in order to help them improve job performance.
Rouziès *et al.* (2017)		x		Perceptions of management fairness have an impact on salespeople's variable-to-total pay in some settings but not in others.	Sales managers in low power distance countries need to show that they are fair. In high power distance countries, such an approach has no benefit.
Arnold *et al.* (2009)	x			There are differentiating effects on salespeople's judgments of the closeness of referents, the level of collectivism in the sales environment, the nature of network ties.	Both under- and over-compensation within a sales organization are detrimental. A group's specific fairness definition is likely to emerge in collective selling environments.

Table 4: Continued

	Fairness Relative to a Referent	Supervisory Fairness	Pay Fairness	Main results pertaining to compensation	Managerial implications
Rouziou et al. (2018b)	x			Salespeople engage in pay comparisons with company top earners. Salespeople who are either lagging far behind or closely approaching the pay of their top colleagues have lower performance levels compared to those in the middle of the pack.	Sales leaders will be better off publicizing the national (local) top earner to segments of salespeople who are (little) highly paid.
Rouziou et al. (2018a)			x	Salespeople's perceptions of pay fairness have a positive effect on salespeople's social capital.	Salespeople are likely to develop stronger social networks and build social capital when sales leaders increase the pay system level of transparency.

is higher when perceived management fairness is high, in low power distance countries (that is where the level of inequality expected and accepted is low). Further, they suggest that in high power distance countries, perceived management fairness does not have any effect on compensation. In other words, fairness does not seem to matter much in countries where salespeople expect inequalities. Such a conclusion indicates that implementing standardized sales force management practices (e.g., promote pay transparency and fairness) may increase productivity less than expected: a topic we will discuss in Chapter 4.

Social Capital. While few scholars studied the impact of salespeople's perceptions of pay fairness, one recent exception includes the study of Rouziou *et al.* (2018a) examining how perceptions of pay fairness can enhance the development of a sales organization's social capital. Their findings indicate that salespeople's social capital can be leveraged to increase sales performance. They find that a climate of pay fairness is likely to induce salespeople to trust and help one another. They further suggest that such a climate is likely to positively influence salespeople's pro-social behavior adoption. Finally, they show that salespeople's perceptions of fairness induces salespeople to strengthen their efforts. Together these results suggest that salespeople's perceptions of fairness are likely to develop their social capital. This is important to know because it means that increasing the level of transparency of sales force's pay system, is likely to induce salespeople to develop stronger social networks and that there may be a virtuous cycle in the network enhancing salespeople's and firm's outcomes.

Targets of Comparisons. Another interesting issue in salespeople's compensation fairness is the question of to whose paychecks do salespeople compare their own? For example, Arnold *et al.* (2009) investigate the role of salespeople's internal and external referents in salespeople's fairness judgments. The authors provide evidence not only for differentiating effects depending on the closeness of referents and the level of network ties but also depending on the level of collectivism in the sales environment. Their results show that salespeople perceive their under-compensation relative to a referent salesperson (internal or external to the firm) to be unfair except in the presence of strong ties in sales environments characterized by high levels of collectivism.

When salespeople are over-compensated, they perceive unfairness only when comparing themselves to salespeople working in their firm in environments characterized by low levels of collectivism. Furthermore, when salespeople use non-sales personnel as referents, they form negative fairness judgments except when comparing their situation to internal non-sales employees when low network ties are developed. Taken together, these results confirm the importance for sales leaders to closely monitor both under- and over-compensation perceptions in their sales organization, especially when these organizations are not tightly knit. Across functional boundaries, the same attention should be devoted to non-sales employees who are used as referents by salespeople. Hence, salespeople may perceive they are not fairly rewarded compared to them except when network ties are weak. To conclude, one key insight of the Arnold *et al.* (2009) study is that comparisons with referents being other salespeople or other employees, within or from outside the firm, impact salespeople's fairness judgments differentially.

Another important issue on the formation of salespeople's fairness judgment derived from their target of compensation comparisons, pertains to salespeople's standing within the organizational pay environment. Typically, salespeople's decision to work may also depend on their assessment of how much they are making *relative* to a comparison referent. Given that salespeople's contributions are generally heterogeneous and that they are often compensated with pay-for-performance (P4P) plans, their pay checks are naturally likely to vary. Drawing on research suggesting that salespeople engage in comparisons with top earners (Wheeler, 1966; Wheeler *et al.*, 1969); Rouziou *et al.* (2018b) examine the impact of salespeople's pay relative to that of a firm's national (inside the whole organization) or local (inside a region) top earners, on performance. In their study, they describe a given salesperson's compensation as being either much smaller, a bit smaller or similar to that of top performers. They find out that salespeople who are either lagging far behind or closely approaching the pay of their top colleagues have lower performance levels compared to those in the middle of the pack. Sales leaders should therefore nurture their core performers (i.e., those salespeople in the middle of the pack), a conclusion similar to that of Ahearne and Steenburgh (2012). In addition, comparisons taking place locally seem to operate differently than comparisons taking place at the national level. Indeed, the aforementioned study finds that comparisons with local top earners are more detrimental to highly paid salespeople whereas comparisons with national top earners are more detrimental to lower paid salespeople. Therefore, business leaders should assess the full impact of pay disparity in sales organizations: publicize national top earners to salespeople who are highly paid and local top earners to lower paid salespeople.

Recent studies also show that top performer rewards may influence other salespeople because of legitimacy issues. According to Miao *et al.* (2017) for example, salespeople may perceive that top performers rewards are not legitimate because they question their competence in terms of customer-relationship building. This is likely to happen when organizational justice is low and sales force behavior control is used. Needless to say that this could be damaging for sales organizations as salespeople may retaliate and behave opportunistically (Miao *et al.*, 2017). Conversely, top-performer rewards may be perceived as legitimate (i.e., when top performers and perceived top-performer customer-relationship-building competence are positively associated) when organizational justice is high and sales force behavior control is employed.

On a broad level, business leaders should assess the full impact of pay disparity in sales organizations. Advertising top earners to other salespeople may not always be beneficial.

3.1.2 Peer Effects

Peer effects have long been studied by economists (e.g., Zimmerman, 2003), psychologists (e.g., Festinger, 1954) and sociologists (e.g., Jencks and Mayer, 1990). In the sales force literature, an emerging path of research investigates the impact of social comparisons and peer effects (e.g., Chan *et al.*, 2014a,b; Miao *et al.*, 2017; Rouziou *et al.*, 2018b) (see Table 5 for a synthesis). For example, to show how salespeople's strategies and outcomes depend on their coworkers, Chan *et al.* (2014a) use data from the cosmetic sales of a large department store over four years. Specifically, they investigate how salespeople's colocation affects their productivity thanks to reorganizations of cosmetic counters, varying task difficulties and financial incentives. Their results are consistent with peer-based learning mechanisms (rather than learning-by-doing effects): lower-ability salespeople increase their sales effectiveness by learning from their higher-ability coworkers in the counters where group-based commissions are used. Further, the authors show that individual financial incentives induce learning effort whereas team-based compensation motivates teaching effort. In addition, they argue that learning from peers is more likely to occur through observation for easier tasks, and through active teaching for more complex ones. Finally, they provide evidence for the crucial impact of star salespeople who enhance peer-based learning for new hires in addition to their own productivity. To retain star salespeople, they conclude that firms should consider offering them additional bonuses.

In a similar sales context, the same authors investigate peer effects (i.e., competing or helping) in sales team under varying compensation systems (Chan *et al.*, 2014b). In keeping with earlier research, they find that salespeople either compete or cooperate with one another depending on the basis of financial incentive allocation (i.e., individual or team-based respectively). Thus, heterogeneous salesforces perform better than homogeneous ones when their financial incentives are based on group sales. Interestingly, the authors find the reverse when salespeople are paid commissions on individual sales (i.e., heterogeneous teams perform worse than homogeneous ones). Specifically, working with salespeople of higher levels of ability within the same firm improves sales productivity in counters where team-based compensation is used, whereas the reverse is true when individual financial incentives are used. Presumably, star salespeople compensated with individual incentives are not only competing with outside peers but also with inside peers. In addition, salespeople compensated with individual financial incentives are more likely than their counterparts compensated with team-based financial incentives, to increase price discounting in response to high-ability peers. All in all, the authors conclude that firms are more likely to benefit from team-based financial incentives. In summary, the results substantiate the belief that salesforces that are heterogeneous in terms of ability should be compensated with team-based compensation as they are likely to enhance their firms' results.

Table 5: Sales force compensation research relaxing the assumption of salespeople's independence (representative studies)

	Learning Processes	Competition or Cooperation	Comparison Costs	Main results pertaining to compensation	Managerial implications
Chan *et al.* (2014a)	x			Lost financial incentives may motivate salespeople to learn from peers instead of learning-by-doing (i.e., experimenting and potentially failing). Higher individual incentives may increase salespeople's learning effort but motivate less their effort toward teaching. In contrast, team-based incentives may motivate salespeople to teach. Star salespeople add value not only through their own productivity but also from enhancing peer-based learning for new hires.	Management should offer additional bonuses to retain star salespeople.

Table 5: Continued

	Learning Processes	Competition or Cooperation	Comparison Costs	Main results pertaining to compensation	Managerial implications
Chan et al. (2014b)		x		Salespeople either compete or cooperate with one another depending on whether they are compensated with individual or team-based financial incentives respectively. Working with salespeople of higher levels of ability within the same firm improves sales productivity when team-based compensation is used whereas the reverse is true when individual financial incentives are used. Salespeople compensated with individual financial incentives are more likely than their counterparts compensated with team-based financial incentives, to increase price discounting in response to high-ability peers.	Salesforces heterogeneous in terms of ability should be compensated with team-based compensation as they are likely to enhance their firms' results.

Table 5: Continued

	Learning Processes	Competition or Cooperation	Comparison Costs	Main results pertaining to compensation	Managerial implications
Miao *et al.* (2017)			x	When overall organizational justice is high and sales force behavior control is employed, top performer rewards are more likely to be perceived as legitimate. When perceived overall organizational justice is low and sales force behavior control is employed, salespeople are much more likely to perceive top-performer rewards as a result of perceived favoritism.	In a sales force behavior control environment, management may ensure that salespeople perceive high levels of overall organizational justice in order to afford the positive effects of top-performer rewards on motivating peers to improve their selling skills.
Rouziou *et al.* (2018b)			x	Salespeople engage in pay comparisons with company top earners. Salespeople who are either lagging far behind or closely approaching the pay of their top colleagues have lower performance levels compared to those in the middle of the pack.	Sales leaders will be better off publicizing the national (local) top earner to segments of salespeople who are (little) highly paid.

3.2   Salespeople and their Careers

As described earlier, the current dominant view in sales force compensation research is based on agency theory. Furthermore, this stream of research focuses mostly on the motivational issue of sales plans (e.g., Basu *et al.*, 1985; Lal and Srinivasan, 1993). While few agency theoretic research studies (e.g., Daljord *et al.*, 2016) emphasize selection and retention issues (Lo *et al.*, 2011), the body of sales force compensation research surprisingly neglects the effect of career paths on compensation. However, the realities of labor markets differ from the vision presented in this literature. In the real world, recruiters generally assess the value of experience to set compensation levels. Given the high turnover rates of the sales profession, this is a fundamental issue for many organizations (Boles *et al.*, 2012).Therefore, studying the effect of career history on compensation is an important research avenue.

Keshavarz *et al.* (2017) are the first to study how firms value sales career paths. Using a unique data set of 76,000 salespeople and 13,000 sales managers' compensation over 17 years, they find that firms invest at a higher rate in sales managers' seniority than in that of salespeople's up to a point after which the marginal returns of seniority decrease at a faster rate for sales managers than for salespeople. Their results confirm that firms value salespeople's firm experience but not industry experience, contrary to conventional wisdom. In addition, they show that sales managers' industry experience is less valued by firms than their sales experience. To conclude, more research is needed to examine the impact of career paths on compensation levels.

3.3   Influence of Culture, JWBs and Religion

Culture dimensions and their potential impact on compensation choices warrant more investigation because companies are increasingly becoming multi-national. Furthermore, the vast majority of research on international compensation are outside the salesforce domain in spite of the central role salespeople play in organizations and the economy of every country (Panagopoulos *et al.*, 2011). It is unthinkable for a company to become multinational without having salesforce that span multiple countries. For example, the top 500 companies in North America employ almost 24 million salespeople across the globe (Chung and Narayandas, 2017). A natural question arises as to how to manage the additional challenges engendered by international and cross-cultural complexities. Given the differences in cultural norms and in social and work-related expectations across countries, decisions about adapting salesforce compensation practices to ensure that salespeople are motivated, regardless of their locations, require a solid foundation.

While there is abundance of research on international compensation, there is a dearth of research on international sales force compensation in spite of the demonstrated importance of this occupational group (Panagopoulos *et al.*, 2011). Notable exceptions include Cravens *et al.* (2006), Hohenberg and Homburg (2016), Liu (1998), Money and Graham (1999), Murphy and Li (2012), and Segalla *et al.* (2006). Most research on international compensation are either comparative (studies comparing aspects of compensation among two or more countries) or MNC-focused (studies examining the compensation systems of multinational corporations). Comparative studies have generally found that there are substantial and important differences in the compensation practices and pay distribution decisions between U.S. and foreign companies. For instance, Gomez-Mejia and Welbourne (1991) argue that MNCs should minimize variable pay in countries with high uncertainty avoidance because managers in such environment tend to focus on risk avoidance and reduction. Consistent with this view, Gooderham *et al.* (1999) found in their multinational study of human resource management practices that German managers employ variable pay system less than their British counterparts do. In addition, Tosi and Greckhamer (2004) reported a negative correlation between the proportion of variable to total CEO compensation and uncertainty avoidance. Other comparative studies have investigated wage inequality, wage systems, pay allocations, gender wage gap, union wages, incentives, and reward expectations across two or more countries (Werner and Ward, 2004).

MNC compensation research has investigated compensation of foreign subsidiaries, expatriates, joint venture, licensing partners and how compensation scheme relate to company valuation and country cultures (Werner and Ward, 2004). This later research reported that for MNCs, foreign posts compensation decisions are more complex than domestic compensation decisions. This greater complexity was attributed to differences in staff mix (locals, expatriates and third-country nationals), host country conditions, national cultures, and exchange rate risk exposures (Werner and Ward, 2004). In their review of compensation research, Werner and Ward (2004) concluded that international compensation was the least researched area. They encouraged scholars to shed more light on areas such as transference of North-America-centric compensation theories, national differences in pay satisfactions, reactions to pay plans, national differences in the importance of pay, pay reactions by locals to expatriate pay, national effects on compensation strategies, and geographical and cultural distance effects on global pay strategies.

Given the increasing number of business leaders who are managing sales teams spread across multiple countries, the rarity of studies on international salesforce management is surprising (Hohenberg and Homburg, 2016; Panagopoulos *et al.*, 2011; Piercy *et al.*, 2011). Granted that empirical data collection for studies involving multiple countries is challenging, this should not hinder the push for academic research to investigate phenomena that are critical to the success of sales organizations as more and more companies become multinational. One aspect of salesforce management that presents an extra layer of challenge is compensation. Not only are data on compensation confidential, but also, monetary matters are sensitive topics that managers usually do not want to discuss publicly so as not to distract the salesforce. Nevertheless, the design and implementation of compensation plans to motivate salespeople operating in different country locations remains a major concern for salesforce leaders as Hohenberg and Homburg (2016) rightfully point out. In this section, we review extant literature on international salesforce compensation, highlighting factors that make international salesforce compensation unique and worthy of more scholarly attention.

3.3.1 Cultural Impact

Scholars have conceptualized culture as a multidimensional construct. These dimensions include individualism and collectivism, masculinity and femininity, uncertainty avoidance, power distance, and long-term orientation (e.g., Hofstede, 1980, 1991, 2001; Hofstede and Bond, 1988).

Individualism is defined as the degree of connectedness among individuals (Hofstede, 1980; Hui and Triandis, 1986). In addition, it is characterized by a preference for financial incentives linked to individual performance (Schuler and Rogovsky, 1998; Tosi and Greckhamer, 2004). Consistently, compensation plans that promote individual performance are prevalent in individualistic cultures.

Masculinity is the degree to which members of a society value challenge, competition, achievement and assertiveness. In contrast, feminine cultures emphasize cooperation and relationship quality. Managers in high masculinity countries tend to show more concern for job performance (Tosi and Greckhamer, 2004) and material possessions (Gomez-Mejia and Welbourne, 1991). Thus, they are more inclined to use incentive compensation. This is consistent with theories of motivation, human resource, and salesforce management, all of which proposed the use of incentive compensation in such settings, encouraging managers to tie behaviors to monetary outcomes (Segalla *et al.*, 2006).

Uncertainty avoidance is the degree to which members of a society accepts risks and not knowing enough about future outcomes. Different cultures exhibit different risk preferences (Weber and Hsee, 1998), in that managers from countries high on cultural uncertainty avoidance would prefer predictable situations, low risk and low ambiguity. For example, Tosi and Greckhamer (2004) found a negative relationship between CEO compensation and uncertainty avoidance. Miller *et al.* (2001) showed that guaranteed rewards based on seniority are more acceptable in countries that exhibit high uncertainty avoidance scores. Gooderham *et al.* (1999) indicated that firms in high uncertainty avoidance countries (e.g., Germany) use incentive reward systems significantly less than firms in low uncertainty avoidance countries (e.g., Great Britain). In addition, Segalla *et al.* (2006) found that German managers are less likely than Anglo-Saxon managers to favor incentive compensation because of the former's higher score on uncertainty avoidance.

Power distance captures the extent to which members of a society accepts inequality (Hofstede, 1980). Managers higher up the hierarchy in high power distance countries enjoy higher status and authority along with financial privileges (Schwartz, 1999; Tosi and Greckhamer, 2004). It has been shown that economic performance is highly valued in high power distance countries because it is considered instrumental to attaining employment security, higher status and authority (Chiang and Birtch, 2012).

Long-term orientation is the degree to which members of a society are willing to sacrifice short-term outcomes for long-term gains. In contrast, people in short-term oriented cultures focus on immediate outcomes and discount future outcomes. Short-term orientation has been used often to characterize salespeople (e.g., Homburg *et al.*, 2008; Kim and McAlister, 2011). Thus, in order to promote long-term orientation, companies use compensation plans that emphasize fixed pay (Cravens *et al.*, 1993; John and Weitz, 1989; Mowen and Mowen, 1991; Oliver and Anderson, 1994).

3.3.2　Country Idiosyncrasies

A generally accepted axiom in salesforce management is that market dynamics (e.g., product life cycle – introduction, growth, maturity, decline – customer types and expectations, level of competition, product portfolio and degree of differentiation, etc.) influence decisions about sales structures which in turn impact decisions about sales roles (tasks and responsibilities). The nature of sales roles drives the profile of salespeople required. Having the right kind and number of salespeople is not enough: salespeople need to be motivated (intrinsically and extrinsically) to invest their skills, knowledge, time, and effort in ways that help the firm achieve its sales objectives. However, the foregoing sequence of influences assume an alignment that is hardly tenable in national and especially international work environments. As such, variance in compensation systems especially in multinational companies should be expected. In fact, salesforce compensation for similar sales roles varies across countries as shown in Tables 1 and 2. However, some companies such as SAP AG, choose to use the same compensation systems for salespeople located in different countries (Cravens *et al.*, 2006; Frank *et al.*, 2015).

There are country idiosyncrasies that make a one-size-fit-all compensation plan difficult to justify. For example, the foreign markets in which MNCs compete do not present the same market dynamic. Hence, the first item in the aforementioned sequence (of decision influence) will differ across countries and this would engender different outcomes in the chain of decisions. Furthermore, placing the entire sequence of inter-related decisions into bigger contexts defined by culture, laws, religion, tax, and data infrastructure introduces additional differences and hence challenges for MNCs (Piercy *et al.*, 2011; Zoltners *et al.*, 2015). Therefore, the idea of having a single compensation plan that is applied uniformly across international markets is difficult to justify and prone to problems (Frank *et al.*, 2015).

Piercy *et al.* (2011) and Zoltners *et al.* (2015) offered several factors that can limit the use of universal salesforce compensation plans. They posit that the following five elements help determine the utility of compensation plans.

Market maturity: salespeople in matured markets tend to focus on customer retention while those in growth markets emphasize customer acquisition. The difference in sales tasks and length of time required makes a universal compensation plan impractical.

Channel structure: since channel structures tend to reflect the way customers buy, in some markets, direct B2B sales (using inside sales and field salesforce) might be the only route to market whereas in other markets, distributors control access to customers. Hence, while salespeople in the latter situation deal with distributors, those in the former deal with end users. These two group of salespeople should not be assessed on the same basis because their roles (and results) are different. It will be problematic paying the two groups of salespeople in the same way.

Business culture: in some countries like China, the collectivist culture encourages teamwork while in other countries like the United States, the individualistic culture encourages individual efforts. Therefore, while individual P4P scheme would be welcomed among salespeople in the latter countries, this type of compensation plan would be resisted in the former (Rouziès *et al.*, 2017; Segalla *et al.*, 2006).

Laws: government regulations and labor unions limit the realm of possibilities in compensation designs. For example, in Brazil, India, France, Japan, and Mexico, government regulations prohibit reductions in base pay. In the case of Brazil, a company cannot transition from fixed pay to variable pay. The law often requires that the fixed pay be maintained alongside the "new" variable pay. In France, a commission-only compensation plan is considered a contract, such that a company cannot change any aspect of the commission (e.g., rate, payment, threshold, and cap) without the explicit and full consent of the salesperson (Proskauer-International HR Best Practices, 2010: www.proskauer.com, page 1). The use of draws against future earnings (a common practice in the United States whereby salespeople on some form of commission plan could receive anticipated payment that will be offset with future earned commission) is illegal under Japanese labor and union laws (Proskauer-International HR Best Practices, 2010: www.proskauer.com). Thus, even when market dynamics favor a particular compensation scheme, the laws of a country might make it unfeasible for a MNC to modify their salesforce compensation plans by reducing the level of fixed salary and increasing the proportion of incentive. In such countries, increasing the proportion of incentives in pay plans will lead to higher salesforce expenditure.

Data availability: the quality of infrastructures around information systems and technology and the willingness to share information directly through data connectivity can enhance or limit the collection of buyer/end user data at the individual salesperson level. Access to such individual level data is sine qua non for the applicability of incentive-based compensation plans. For example, whereas a Multinational corporation could easily implement individual-level incentive compensation among its salesforce in the United States, it could not do so in Nigeria for lack of individual level end user sales data.

Accordingly, it is unrealistic to expect that a single, uniform salesforce compensation plan would be effective globally (Piercy *et al.*, 2011; Zoltners *et al.*, 2015). In a study of salesforce management practices using data from nine countries (Austria, Greece, Bahrain, Saudi Arabia, India, Israel, Malaysia, Nigeria, and United Kingdom), Cravens *et al.* (2006) found that all aspects except one (the use of incentive compensation) reflected similarities across the countries studied. They attributed the differences in the use and consequences of incentive compensation to differences in cultural, economic and socio-political characteristics of the countries. Interestingly, the authors assumed there is compelling and increasing evidence of global convergence of sales management practices. They mentioned SAP AG's replacement of its country-based incentive program with a global one in 50 countries. They continued, "SAP and other firms are learning that similarities across countries and making the old way of regional or local management control less effective in today's global business environment," (Cravens *et al.*, 2006, p. 291), citing arguments in Thomas Friedman's bestseller *The World is Flat* to support their claim. While they found support for most of their hypotheses, no support was found for the global use of P4P schemes. Yet again, one-size-fits-all approach in international salesforce compensation does not work.

Companies can in principle use information about market dynamics and country laws to conclude about the suitability of a salesforce compensation scheme. However, this does not guarantee the acceptability of the compensation scheme by members of the sales force. In a recent review, Frank *et al.* (2015) concluded that business leaders and managers are realizing that not all pay and compensation systems are equally acceptable around the world. For example, Walmart's failure in Germany was partly attributed to the company's unwillingness to adopt egalitarian German wage-setting practices (Frank *et al.*, 2015). Similarly, Lincoln Electric failed initially in its international expansion (from the United States) because the company's managers incorrectly assumed that all cultures were equally receptive to Lincoln's P4P system (Hastings, 1999). Furthermore, the growing international debate about income inequality (Piketty, 2014; Plender, 2012) challenges the acceptability across cultures of high-powered individual performance incentives, a prevalent practice in salesforce organizations. Surprisingly, the foregoing phenomenon has generated very limited research enquiry in the management literature. One would have thought that the prevalence of P4P scheme in salesforce organizations would attract the focus of management scholars to study whether and why acceptability of compensation systems vary across individual salespeople working in the same organization but in different cultures. Frank *et al.* (2015) provided an elaborate theoretical foundation for explaining cross-cultural variances in preferences for incentive compensation that we describe next.

3.3.3   Cultural Differences in JWB

Frank *et al.* (2015) posit that cultural differences in acceptability of individual-level compensation plans are partly caused by cultural differences in JWBs. JWBs "refer to individual's general beliefs about whether the world is a fair place where people largely get what they deserve (Lerner, 1980)" (Frank *et al.*, 2015, p.160). Specifically, whereas in cultures where JWBs are strong, employees would perceive individual P4P as fair, motivating, and desirable, in cultures where JWBs are weak, employees would perceive individual P4P as unfair, demotivating, and undesirable. In the latter situation, employees would prefer more re-distributive, equal payment plans. In other words, "strong JWBs imply that people see a strong positive correlation between effort and success, whereas weak JWBs imply that people do not see a clear relationship between effort and success" (Frank *et al.*, 2015, p. 161). In their first study, the authors showed that individual preferences for P4P plans correlated with JWBs in a culturally diverse sample of professionally experienced graduate students. In the second study, they found that American undergraduate participants had stronger preferences than French undergraduates did for using performance-based metrics to determine their own individual payment for an experimental task. In a final study, the researchers confirmed that JWBs constitute the psychological mechanism that causes cultural differences in preferences for economic redistribution. None of the international salesforce compensation studies conducted till date directly or explicitly evoked the notion of JWBs. However, although the hypotheses developed in Frank *et al.* (2015) were tested in controlled experiments using student subjects, the findings provide many interesting insights that could be leveraged for international salesforce compensation research. More importantly, the theoretical underpinning of the research can be leveraged by sales force compensation researchers.

Although published almost two decades before Frank *et al.* (2015), Liu (1998) implicitly alluded to the theoretical mechanism proposed by Frank *et al.* (2015) in investigating cross-cultural effectiveness of salesforce reward systems among Chinese salespeople in Mainland China and their counterparts in Hong Kong. After the collapse of communist regimes in Europe and other parts of the world, many multinational firms opened sales operations in former socialist markets and staffed these operations with local salespeople. Even countries like China whose economy remained predominantly socialist opened their doors to western multinational corporations. With the expansion of Hong Kong businesses into mainland China in the 90s, sales managers wanted to know if the compensation systems used for Hong Kong Chinese salespeople are appropriate for Mainland Chinese salespeople. Although Mainland China and Hong Kong share a Chinese cultural heritage, they have been under Eastern and Western influence respectively. Specifically, the values of Hong Kong Chinese metamorphosed under British colonial rule.

The author found that whereas Mainland China salespeople prefer group-oriented reward and rewards that minimize variances across salespeople, Hong Kong salespeople prefer individual-based reward systems like variable compensation and do not mind having large variances in compensation across salespeople in the same company. The author theoretically attributed this difference in preferences to differences in power distance and individualism between the two countries. The study concluded that salespeople under the influence of different cultures have different reward perceptions and preferences.

In a similar study published around the same time, Money and Graham (1999, p. 158) posited that "in cultures where individualism and economics are highly valued, individual characteristics such as education, valence for pay, and performance, will be salient. Alternatively, in cultures where collective effort and personal relationships and status are highly valued, organization-related variables such as seniority and value congruence will be more salient." Their results showed that what motivates the U.S. salespeople differs from what motivates the Japanese salespeople. They also reported that individual financial incentives are not the recommended practice in Japan. They concluded, "If the trends in globalization suggest hiring local salespeople who are most familiar with the culture of the country of the target market, it would also suggest that the practice of recruiting, training and motivating those personnel should be different as well" (p. 168).

Murphy and Li (2012) used data from 888 salespeople in Canada, Mexico, United States, China, Australia, and New Zealand to show that salespeople in highly masculine countries are more motivated by incentive pay schemes. In one of the most recent studies of salesforce incentive compensation across multiple countries, Hohenberg and Homburg (2016) investigated the response of salespeople to various approaches aimed at motivating innovation selling (i.e., the selling of new-to-the-world or new-to-the-category products). As part of the study, they examined how 406 salespeople who work for an international B2B supplier and based in 38 countries react to the use of financial incentives to motivate innovation selling. Their results show that salesforce steering instruments (e.g., variable compensation) should be aligned with salesperson national culture measured by power distance, individualism, uncertainty avoidance, and long-term orientation. For example, they found that the total effect on salesperson performance (i.e., sales of innovations) increased by more than 350 percent when firms used variable compensation in high individualistic (versus less individualistic) cultures.

Put together, the foregoing findings strongly suggest that sales force compensation schemes should be customized to local contexts, taking into account the idiosyncrasies of countries where multinational corporations operate. Doing so would be consistent with survey data showing that the same sales job are compensated differently in different countries (Tables 1 and 2). A global guideline to assist multinational corporations in motivating their salespeople, regardless of their locations, can only be drafted if more research are conducted. Such research should bring multiple theoretic lenses to bear on research questions about cross-country sales force compensation. However, several scholars (e.g., Piercy *et al.*, 2011; Rouziès *et al.*, 2009; Segalla *et al.*, 2006; Zoltners *et al.*, 2015) have suggested antidotes to the challenges of designing and implementing salesforce compensation plans that span international boundaries. These include:

a) Develop global guidelines anchored on the firm's strategic goals and sufficiently flexible to enable local managers adapt to local realities (e.g., taxes) in the pursuit of the firm's strategic goals.

b) Create a compensation center that houses continuously curated global best practices, experiences, wisdom, and support staff to disseminate, train, advice, and support local managers in the design and implementation of salesforce compensation plans.

c) Centralized administration of compensation plans in order to reduce costs, gain efficiencies from scale economy, and minimize distractions from the most important tasks of actually selling and managing the salesforce.

d) MNCs should anticipate this trend and be proactive about communicating their salesforce compensation practices, explaining the basis of salesforce compensation and providing rationale for differences when these exist.

The theoretical frameworks that have guided international compensation research require further validation in different empirical contexts. Thus, the practitioner community needs guidance in view of the accelerating pace of mergers and acquisitions.

3.3.4 Religion Specificities

If research at the crossroads of culture and sales force compensation is scarce, investigation of the sensitivity of sales force compensation to religious beliefs is practically non-existent (for a recent exception see Onyemah *et al.*, 2018). Again, like in the case of cultural influences in compensation schemes, sales force scholars will need to look outside the sales force literature for advances in compensation studies involving religion. Beyond investigating the impact of culture on compensation practices, research into the role played by religion in business decisions has started to gain grounds. Although no study examining the consequences of religion has yet been published in the sales force literature, we posit that the insights so far generated from other business disciplines (Gundolf and Filser, 2013) could be leveraged to study its impact on sales force management practices, especially in the area of compensation.

Religion encompasses attitudes and behaviors by individuals with respect to what, in their opinion, transcends reality (Saroglou and Cohen, 2011). These attitudes and behaviors inform the individuals' philosophy of life and hence the manner in which they interpret and respond to phenomena. Religiosity is increasingly considered to be an important contextual construct (Chan-Serafin, 2013; Hilary and Hui, 2009), having direct and indirect implications for attitudes and behaviors of employees. Ronen and Shenkar (2013, p. 871) postulate that "religion may be part of culture, constitute culture, include and transcend culture, be influenced by culture, shape culture, or interact with culture in influencing cognitions and emotions; however, religion does not equal culture, and culture does not necessarily include religion." These ideas suggest that religion and culture are distinct but related constructs (Ronen and Shenkar, 2013; Saroglou and Cohen, 2011).

Some scholars have examined the relationship between religiosity and various managers' characteristics, for example, suggesting a positive relationship between individual religiosity and risk aversion (Hilary and Hui, 2009; Miller and Hoffman, 1995). At an aggregate level, this link has been found to impact organizational behavior; in particular, Hilary and Hui (2009) found that firms located in counties (in the U.S.) with higher levels of religiosity exhibited lesser risk exposure, growth and investment rate but commanded more positive market reaction when they announced new investments. As Hilary and Hui (2009, p. 455) state, "firms do not make decisions, people do and what they do outside work is likely to affect the ways they make these decisions inside work." The reference to risk aversion in the aforementioned studies provides a motivation to investigate sales force compensation under different levels of religiosity. Specifically, since the use of incentive compensation is common in sales settings, salespeople face uncertainties with regards to their pay and hence it is plausible that their attitude towards this uncertainty would be influenced by their religiosity. More so, their acceptance of a compensation plan, in the case that the plan has a variable or semi-variable component that is contingent on actual performance (which is a priori unknown because of market uncertainties) might vary depending on their religious orientation.

Faith and hope, together with charity, are fundamental to the world's largest religions. While some people might naturally have a low tolerance for ambiguity, this disposition should be mitigated as they become more fervent in their religious beliefs (Lechner *et al.*, 2015). In attempting to be all encompassing and/or, sophisticated, sales organizations end up with complex formulas for computing incentive compensation. Presumably, such complex plans hinder impact because lack of clarity or knowledge undermines engagement.

3.4 Emerging Sales Force Compensation Research Based on Unique Data Sets

Recently, a new sales force compensation research stream has emerged (see Table 6 for a summary). Thanks to unique data sets, scholars are now able to investigate a wider range of real-world compensation plans. Recent and important findings based on the analysis of such micro-level company data indicate that some widely-used compensation practices such as capping total pay or ratcheting quotas (i.e., raising quotas if salespeople have exceeded them the previous year) may in fact hurt sales (Chung, 2015). This is what Misra and Nair (2011) found in their interesting study of a company's compensation plan featuring a fixed salary and commissions earned over quotas and capped to prevent salespeople from earning too much. Using numerical dynamic programming techniques, the authors model salespeople's reactions to these standard compensation policies (i.e., caps and ratcheting). They show and demonstrate –through the field implementation of their recommended plan in the company– that a better compensation plan features low quotas, no ceiling and monthly commissions. Indeed, their proposed plan improves the focused company's sales revenues by 9 percent. Interestingly, with the proposed plan, gaming disappears.

In the same vein, Chung *et al.* (2014) provide rich insights for sales academics and leaders: they assess the reactions of salespeople (at different performance levels) to various compensation plan elements thanks to real company data. Using a dynamic structural model of salespeople response to compensation elements (i.e., salary, commissions, lump-sum bonuses for achieving quotas, and different commission rates beyond achieving quotas), they suggest different strategies to improve the focal firm's performance. Specifically, in order to keep the best performers engaged, the authors suggest to use overachievement commissions.

Table 6: Sales force compensation research based on field experiments (representative studies)

	Main results pertaining to compensation	Managerial implications
Chung *et al.* (2014)	The authors suggest different strategies depending on salespeople's performance levels to improve the focal firm's performance. Specifically, in order to keep the best performers engaged, the authors suggest to use overachievement commissions. Similarly, in order to keep low performers motivated at every step along the way, they propose to use quarterly bonuses.	Sales leaders should take into account the heterogeneity of their salesforce. They should use quarterly bonuses for weak performers and overachievement commissions for high performers.
Chung and Narayandas (2017)	Conditional compensation (i.e., quota bonus incentives) improves performance but may lower future performance. It is also effective across various types of salespeople. Unconditional compensation (i.e., bonus payment regardless of performance) improves performance if it is given as a delayed reward but becomes less effective with time. It is more effective for salespeople with high base performance.	Sales leaders should use conditional compensation in a highly competitive market to increase short term rather than long term performance. Sales leaders should use unconditional compensation for salespeople with higher-level selling skills.

Table 6: Continued

	Main results pertaining to compensation	Managerial implications
Dustin and Belasen (2013)	Impact of a compensation reduction on salespeople's performance over time: salespeople at high pay levels change their effort less than their counterparts at lower pay levels.	Sales leaders can reduce salespeople's compensation programs without decreasing performance for salespeople whose pay is tightly linked to performance, providing their pay is relatively high compared to salespeople working for other firms in the same market.
Misra and Nair (2011)	Using dynamic-programming based agency theory models will allow sales leaders to assess and improve their sales-force compensation schemes providing they are no buyer-side demand dynamics or seasonality.	Standard compensation policies (i.e., caps and ratcheting) may hurt a company's performance. A better compensation plan may feature low quotas, no ceiling and monthly commissions.

Likewise, in order to keep low performers motivated at every step along the way, they propose to use quarterly bonuses.

In addition to using company data, this new stream of research features field experiments. As described above (see Section 3.1.2), studies such as Chan *et al.* (2014a,b) include quasi-experiments to demonstrate the importance of considering peer interactions when designing compensation plans. Other scholars are also comparing groups of salespeople's effort and performance in response to their assigned pay structures and levels. For example, Dustin and Belasen (2013) examine the impact of a compensation reduction on salespeople's performance over time. Conducting a quasi-experiment interrupted time-series design to rule out alternative explanations, they confirm that salespeople increase their level of performance when faced with a compensation reduction in order to maintain their level of pay. Further, they show that this phenomenon is stronger at lower, rather than higher, levels of pay.

Using a randomized field experiment, other researchers such as Chung and Narayandas (2017) also investigate salespeople's reactions to various compensation schemes. They provide rich and insightful results. They confirm the effectiveness of quota-bonus incentives across all types of salespeople. Further, they show how unconditional compensation (i.e., bonus regardless of performance) improves salespeople's performance, especially those with high base performance. However, the improvement magnitude is less than half that of the conditional bonus plan. In addition, unconditional bonuses seem to work when allocated as delayed rewards.

These emerging research trends allow investigations of new territories such as peer effects, social comparisons or careers. Let us hope that more scholars will continue examine other novel and under-researched concepts in sales force compensation.

4

Managerial Implications and Directions for Future Research

4.1 Practical Advice to Managers

Companies reassess their compensation plans periodically not only because sales environments are dynamic but also in order to improve their performance (Zoltners *et al.*, 2006, p. 40). However, they need guidance for such frequent and crucial decisions. The reviews covered in this manuscript already offered many practical suggestions for designing and managing sales force compensation. For example,

a) Sales managers need to be more transparent with their compensation practices and spend more time with salespeople in order to help them improve job performance. This is because increasing the level of transparency of sales force's pay system would minimize unfair criticisms and help salespeople focus their attention on the job.

b) Widely-used compensation practices such as capping total pay or ratcheting quotas (i.e., raising quotas that were exceeded in previous year) may in fact hurt sales.

c) Sales managers should consider using overachievement commissions to keep the best performers engaged and quarterly bonuses to keep low performers motivated.

We go beyond these suggestions and offer some guidance in subsequent paragraphs.

Sales force compensation planning should involve leaders from different functional areas.

The saying that "nothing happens until someone sells something" suggests that the way salespeople are compensated affects every part of an organization (marketing, engineering, production, human resources, logistics, accounting, finance, and legal department). This is because salespeople's success at communicating, delivering and extracting customer value depends on every part of the organization working seamlessly together towards a common goal. While the company's sales leaders should lead salesforce compensation design and implementation, inputs from other areas of the company are critical to achieving an effective sales force compensation that fosters collaborative climate and enables salespeople to get the support they need to fulfill promises made to customers.

Customize salesforce compensation to fit sales roles.

At a macro level, several design principles are recommended. Firstly, when sales tasks are highly programmable and the importance of non-selling task is high, the use of salary is recommended (e.g., Anderson, 1985; John and Weitz, 1989). Secondly, the use of salary is recommended for smaller salesforces because such small-size salesforces make it possible to have lower control span and closer monitoring. Thirdly, a greater use of salary compensation is recommended the more difficult it is to measure individual salesperson performance. Fourthly, a greater use of salary compensation is consistent with behavior control philosophies while incentives are recommended where outcome control philosophies are in place.

At a micro level, no two sales roles are the same. Sales roles can be characterized by the type of customers served, length of sales cycle, strategic sales objective (e.g., customer acquisition versus customer retention, growth versus consolidation, profitability/margin versus sales volume/market share), type of sales (e.g., virtual sales versus face-to-face sales, inside sales versus field sales), stages in the sales process (e.g., lead generation and qualification versus proposal presentation and closing), and basis of selling (e.g., individual versus team selling).

Given the differences in knowledge, skill, effort, time, and expectations associated with different sales roles, compensation (i.e., pay level, pay mix, payout function, etc.) should be tailored accordingly. The array of possibilities is such that a one-size-fits-all compensation plan may be very difficult to achieve.

Adapt sales force compensation plans to country specific idiosyncrasies.

Multinational corporations face a layer of differences in addition to the differences engendered by various sales roles. The same sales role might need to be compensated differently in different countries because of possibilities offered or restrictions imposed by national labor and tax laws. Furthermore, the same product might be in different stages (i.e., product life cycle) of market development across countries, thus requiring different sales goals and approaches. Finally, sales force compensation plans should reflect cultural norms of the society in which the company salesforce operate.

Caution when borrowing or copying compensation plans.

Consistent with the fact that there is no one-size-fits-all sales force compensation plans whether at the company-, or country level, companies should exercise caution when imitating sales force compensation plans from other companies. This is because companies must assess their context (i.e., sales structure, sales roles, sales objectives, market location, etc.) carefully before deciding on the appropriate way to compensate their salesforce. Every salesforce compensation plan is idiosyncratic to the circumstances and needs of the company that designs and implements it.

Social comparison of salesforce compensation plans.

The prevalence of social media and the emergence of pay comparison organizations like Glassdoor.com make it easier for peers to access and share information about pay. Unfavorable outcomes from pay comparison generate tension, sense of unfairness, demotivation, and dissatisfaction with pay, supervisors, and employer. These may also lead to staff turnover. Companies should be transparent and communicate proactively about their sales force compensation plans and more importantly, the basis of such plans. Doing so routinely will minimize the risk of unfair and erroneous pay comparisons by peers.

Monitor and evaluate compensation plans periodically.

Changes in market dynamics could trigger changes to sales structure and roles. These changes could make obsolete existing salesforce compensation plans. The exit and/or, entry of competitors in some territories or markets could necessitate a redefinition of sales territories, which in turn affects variable compensation. In addition, changes in labor and tax laws could require tweaks to existing compensation plans. In general, the monitoring of operating environment and assessing alignment between this and existing compensation plans should be conducted periodically. Immediate actions should be taken to address misalignments as consequences may seriously undermine company's performance.

Compensation is an important but not the only source of salesforce motivation.

According to 2017 Gallup polls, 50 percent of employees who quit cite their manager as the reason. Thus while the pay might be good, the quality of relationship between bosses and their subordinates and the quality of leadership provided affect employee motivation and engagement. Sales results, whether positive or negative, might be unrelated to sales force compensation. There are employees willing to forgo more pay for better work environments. Excessive focus on compensation to solve sales problems wrongly assumes the "it's all about money" mindset. Compensation alone cannot be used to obtain retention because there will always be organizations capable of offering high pay.

4.2   Avenues for Research

This monograph clearly suggests that there is an urgent need to generate more insights on the topic of sales force compensation. Guiding questions could include the issues described below:

Careers. As explained earlier, more research effort on sales careers and compensation is needed in the future. Today, a number of questions related to sales careers remain unanswered. It is important to know more about the value of sales careers because compensation budgets typically represent the biggest marketing budget of B2B companies. When firms are hiring sales personal, it would be interesting to shed light on the career characteristics firms are paying for: are they valuing specific trajectories? Presumably experience in marketing or technical jobs before moving into sales jobs should be better rewarded than experience in sales only because marketing and technical skills are generally needed to sell. We could also argue that high performers are better off switching company as employers tend to take into account their earlier training investments when setting compensation levels. More to the point, hardly any research has addressed the promotion decisions in sales organizations. As a result, we still do not know what is the profile of employees who become sales managers, or the profile of salespeople who never become sales managers. All in all, research on these and related questions would provide useful insights.

Interfaces.

Inside-outside sales people and online channels. As sales organizations are evolving towards sales structures involving inside and outside sales together with an e-commerce channel, it would be useful to test different types of compensation plans so that inside and outside salespeople coordinate their efforts with the online channel to enhance the value cocreated with their customers. A tentative quota/bonus plan where bonuses are shared across the three channels could be investigated over several time periods. More generally, a line of inquiry investigating the compensation of these new sales organizational structures is strongly needed.

Functional Interfaces. In keeping with Midgley (2013, p. 147), we also argue that research should investigate the issue of sales and marketing interface through the compensation lens. More specifically, scholars should study the process successful firms use to get (incentives-driven) sales and (salaried) marketing employees work together. This is especially interesting since salespeople choose jobs/incentives that fit their ability/risk aversion (Lo *et al.*, 2011). For example, Rouziès and Hulland (2014) investigate how relationships between marketing and sales may facilitate the development of social capital associated with value creation. However, they did not examine thoroughly the impact of each functional group compensation. We could argue that in firms where important pay gaps exist between sales and marketing employees, successful relationships entail specific types of environment (such as organizations where marketing holds little influence as compared to sales).

Interestingly, similar investigations could be carried out with other functional groups (i.e., R&D, finance, logistics, etc.) than marketing as salespeople need to interact with counterparts from other functional units. To the best of our knowledge, there is no research on gaps existing between sales compensation and finance, marketing, R&D compensation for example. Since sales employees interact with many different functions to better serve their customers, it is unlikely that compensation gaps have no effect on functional alignment or firm performance. Intuitively, we can expect social comparisons to take place. Studies that measure these cross-functional comparisons and their resulting impact would provide useful insights.

Field Testing. Experts on both practical (e.g., O'Connell and Blessington, 2018) and theoretical (e.g., Chung and Narayandas, 2017) fronts call for more field tests of compensation plans. Indeed, this research methodology would allow managers and researchers to assess the performance of specific types of compensation scheme and check underlying assumptions. There has already been calls to test conditional vs. unconditional variable sales compensation in long-sales cycles, quota amounts with bonus levels and time horizons, individual or group bonuses, bases for commissions (i.e., profit, gross margin, market share, etc.), cash vs. noncash compensation (i.e., merchandise or other symbolic incentives such as training programs), the ratio of fixed vs. incentive compensation, compensation caps or quota ratcheting. Other topics related to compensation include that of sales force organization. Indeed, there remains many unanswered questions regarding the relationship between compensation and the level of performance heterogeneity in a sales force. For example, various types of team/individual financial incentives could be tested depending on the weight of "rookies" in a sales force. Similar field tests could be conducted to explore the relationship between sales-force specialization and compensation. In other words, future research could investigate compensation schemes that can accomodate specialists and generalists salespeople in the same firm. We could add to this list, assumptions related to the level of complexity/sophistication of compensation plans: experts recommend limiting the number of objectives to 4 or 5 but this, to the best of our knowledge, has never been tested. Needless to say that all the above topics should also be tested across cultures.

5

Conclusion

Practitioners and researchers alike recognize the importance of sales force compensation. Practitioners need more guidance and the emergence of new streams of research on this topic is a good sign that they will get more help. As described earlier, scholars fruitfully examined compensation plans using several theoretical lenses. The body of sales force compensation research in the field of marketing based on agency theory is the most prolific one, however, this self-contained literature develops insights that are difficult to test and apply to many selling situations, given the many restrictive assumptions discussed earlier (e.g. salespeople independence, time orientation). In other words, sales force compensation research has not kept pace with recent development trends (e.g., development of online, inside and outside sales channels, international expansion, social selling).

Hence, the increasing pace of globalization, mergers and acquisitions and technological developments is forcing the mobility of labor across national boundaries as companies struggle to transfer knowledge and harmonize their organizational culture. Improved virtual collaboration platforms (internet, Skype, Zoom, GoTo Meeting) and teleconferencing capabilities have facilitated the exchange of information and encouraged joint project by virtual teams. In the case of sales organizations, it is now easier to form virtual sales teams that could leverage individual local expertise to sell to multinational buyers who require product and service delivery aligned with local realities. Furthermore, social media platforms such as LinkedIn and Facebook have made it easier to make connections (intra- and inter-company). On these platforms, information (confidential or not) are shared freely. Thus, it is easier for salespeople to acquire information about working conditions (e.g., roles, territories, workload, and compensation) of their colleagues in the same company or in competing organizations. This development is putting pressure on sales managers and management to be transparent. The prevalence of digital marketing channels (e.g., e-commerce platforms) has empowered not only business-to-consumer buyers but also B2B buyers by providing easier access to comparative product knowledge that could be used to define request for proposals, assess proposals, and make purchase decisions.

Furthermore, purchase decisions are increasingly team-based and salespeople will have to make compelling argument to every member of the decision making team. Doing this will often require that the salesperson goes to sales meetings together with his/her colleagues from engineering, customer support, and top management to increase the likelihood that all buyer concerns and objections will be effectively addressed. This means increased level of task interdependency because salespeople will have to build coalition within his/her own company and work with people from various units inside buyer organizations (Bradford *et al.*, 2010). Basically, B2B sales is more complex than ever because of the increased number of people, influences, interactions involved. Attributing sales success to the effort of a single individual (e.g., the salesperson) is less tenable.

This conclusion calls into question the very notion of individual-based incentive pay. The combined influence of the larger and immediate environment ("Environment" and "Context" in Figure 2) thus creates challenges with respect to the assessment of salespeople's efforts, results, and rewards especially when salespeople work for the same company but in different international locations. Organizations will have to be more careful with their salesforce compensation plans

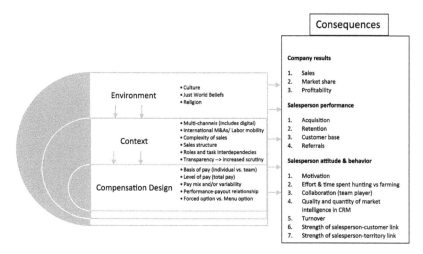

Figure 2: A compensation design model.

because: (1) Information about salespeople pay in different companies is available online (e.g., glassdoor.com) and (2) Salespeople discuss their compensation (basis, mix, percentages, and actual amount) on social media.

When salespeople possess information about how their colleagues in the same company but in different countries are paid, it is inevitable that they engage in social comparison. This comparison could engender negative feelings if for example there is perception of unfairness or injustice. Moreover, this could lead to frustration, demotivation, disruptive behavior, sabotage, or turnover. Therefore, the recent emerging trends featuring new methodologies (i.e., natural or field experiments) and the exploration of virgin territories (i.e., international compensation plans, salespeople's social comparisons, and salespeople's career paths) appear full of promise. We hope this monograph will help researchers and practitioners to collaborate in order to shed more light on some of the pressing issues.

Acknowledgements

The authors wish to thank Dawn Iacobucci (Vanderbilt University) who first encouraged this project, Michael Segalla (HEC Paris) for his detailed and constructive feedback, as well as Koenraad Klaes and Frédéric Lhereec (Korn and Ferry – Hay Group) for many valuable conversations and for providing the unique data sets presented in Tables 1 and 2. The authors also thank the editor and the reviewers for their guidance in the review process.

This work was supported by the EDF Chair at HEC Paris and by a public grant overseen by the French National Research Agency (ANR) as part of the "*Investissements d'Avenir*" program (ANR-11-IDEX-0003/Labex Ecodec/ANR-11-LABX-0047).

References

Adams, J. S. (1965). "Inequity in Social Exchange". In: *Advances in Experimental Social Psychology*. Ed. by L. Berkowitz. Vol. 2. New York: Academic Press.

Adamson, B., M. Dixon, and N. Toman (2013). "Dismantling the Sales Machine". *Harvard Business Review*: 102–109. November.

Ahearne, M. (2017). "Research Centers, Business Schools, and the World of Sales". *Journal of the Academy of Marketing Science*. 45: 461–464.

Ahearne, M. and T. Steenburgh (2012). "Motivating Salespeople: What Really Works". *Harvard Business Review*: 71–75. July–August.

Anderson, E. (1985). "Contracting the Selling Function: The Salesperson as an Outside Agent or Employee". *Marketing Science*. 4(Summer): 234–254.

Anderson, E. and R. L. Oliver (1987). "Perspectives on Behavior-Based Versus Outcome-Based Sales Force Control Systems". *Journal of Marketing*. 51: 76–88.

Arnold, T. J., T. D. Landry, L. K. Scheer, and S. Stan (2009). "The Role of Equity and Work Environment in the Formation of Salesperson Distributive Fairness Judgments". *Journal of Personal Selling & Sales Management*. 29(1): 61–80.

Aryee, S., F. O. Walumbwa, R. Mondejar, and C. W. L. Chu (2015). "Accounting for the Influence of Overall Justice on Job Performance: Integrating Self-Determination and Social Exchange Theories". *Journal of Management Studies*. 52(2): 231–252.

Basu, A., R. Lal, V. Srinivasan, and R. Staelin (1985). "Salesforce Compensation Plans: An Agency Theoretic Perspective". *Marketing Science*. 4: 267–291.

Boles, J., G. Dudley, V. Onyemah, D. Rouziès, and B. Weeks (2012). "Sales Force Turnover and Retention: A Research Agenda". *Journal of Personal Selling & Sales Management*. 32(1): 131–140. Winter.

Bradford, K., S. Brown, S. Ganesan, G. Hunter, V. Onyemah, R. Palmatier, D. Rouziès, R. Spiro, H. Sujan, and B. A. Weitz (2010). "The Embedded Salesforce: Connecting Buying and Selling Organizations". *Marketing Letters*. 21(3): 239–253.

Chan, T. Y., J. Li, and L. Pierce (2014a). "Learning from Peers: Knowledge Transfer and Sales Force Productivity Growth". *Marketing Science*. 33(4): 463–484.

Chan, T. Y., J. Li, and L. Pierce (2014b). "Compensation and Peer Effects in Competing Sales Teams". *Management Science*. 60(8): 1965–1984.

Chan-Serafin, S. (2013). "How Does Religion Matter and Why? Religion and the Organizational Sciences". *Organization Science*. 24(5): 1585–1600.

Chiang, F. F. T. and T. A. Birtch (2012). "The Performance Implications of Financial and Non-Financial Rewards: An Asian Nordic Comparison". *Journal of Management Studies*. 49(3): 538–570. May.

Chung, D. J. (2015). "How to Really Motivate Salespeople". *Harvard Business Review*. 93(4): 54–61. April.

Chung, D. J. and D. Narayandas (2017). "Incentives Versus Reciprocity: Insights from a Field Experiment". *Journal of Marketing Research*. 54(August): 511–524.

Chung, D. J., T. Steenburgh, and K. Sudhir (2014). "Do Bonuses Enhance Sales Productivity? A Dynamic Structural Analysis of Bonus-Based Compensation Plans". *Marketing Science*. 33(2): 165–187.

Churchill Jr., G. A., N. M. Ford, S. W. Hartley, and O. C. Walker Jr (1985). "The Determinants of Salesperson Performance: A Meta-Analysis". *Journal of Marketing Research.* 22(May): 103–118.

Colquitt, J. A., D. E. Conlon, M. J. Wesson, P. Cohl, and N. Ky (2001). "Justice at the Millennium: a Meta-Analytic Review of 25 Years of Justice Research". *Journal of Applied Psychology.* 86(3): 424–445.

Coughlan, A. T. and K. Joseph (2014). *Sales Force Compensation: Research Insights and Research Potential.* Edward Elgar Publishing Ltd. 473–495.

Coughlan, A. T. and C. Narasimhan (1992). "An Empirical Analysis of Sales-Force Compensation Plans". *Journal of Business.* 65(1): 93–121.

Coughlan, A. T. and S. Sen (1989). "Salesforce Compensation: Theory and Managerial Implications". *Marketing Science.* 8: 324–342.

Cravens, D. W., N. F. Piercy, and G. S. Low (2006). "Globalization of the Sales Organization: Management Controls and its Consequences". *Organizational Dynamics.* 35(3): 291–303.

Cravens, D. W., R. W. L. Thomas N. Ingram, and C. A. Young (1993). "Behavior-Based and Outcome-Based Salesforce Control Systems". *Journal of Marketing.* 57(4): 47–59.

Daljord, Ø., S. Misra, and H. S. Nair (2016). "Homogeneous Contracts for Heterogeneous Agents: Aligning Sales Force Composition and Compensation". *Journal of Marketing Research.* 53: 161–182.

Darmon, R. Y. (1974). "Salesmen's Response to Financial Incentives: An Empirical Study". *Journal of Marketing Research.* 11(4): 418–426.

Day, R. L. and P. D. Bennett (1962). "Should Salesmen's Compensation Be Geared to Profits?" *Journal of Marketing.* 26(October): 69.

Deloitte and Oracle (2008). "Strategic Sales Compensation Survey". URL: http://www.oracle.com/us/corporate/press/015200_EN (accessed on 10/05/2108).

Delves Broughton, P. (2012). "Selling Deserves a Corner Office". *Financial Times.* May 1, 14.

Dustin, S. L. and A. R. Belasen (2013). "The Impact of Negative Compensation Changes on Individual Sales Performance". *Journal of Personal Selling & Sales Management.* 33(4): 403–417.

Eisenhardt, K. M. (1985). "Control: Organizational and Economic Approaches". *Management Science*. 31: 134–49.

Eisenhardt, K. M. (1988). "Agency and Institutional Explanations of Compensation in Retail Sales". *Academy of Management Journal*. 31: 488–511.

Eurostat (2009). "European Union Labour Force Survey". URL: http://ec.europa.eu/employment_social/eie/statistical_annex_key _employment_indicators_en.html and http://appsso.eurostat.ec. europa.eu/nui/submitViewTableAction.do (accessed on 07/20/2017).

Falk, A., E. Fehr, and C. Zehnder (2006). "Fairness Perceptions and Reservation Wages–the Behavioral Effects of Minimum Wage Laws". *Quarterly Journal of Economics*. 121(4): 1347–1381.

Festinger, L. (1954). "A Theory of Social Comparison Processes". *Human Relations*. 7: 117–140.

Frank, D. H., K. Wertenbroch, and W. W. Maddux (2015). "Performance Pay or Redistribution? Cultural Differences in Just-World Beliefs and Preferences for Wage Inequality". *Organizational Behavior and Human Decision Processes*. 130: 160–170.

Fredrickson, J. W., A. Davis-Blake, and W. G. Sanders (2010). "Sharing the Wealth: Social Comparisons and Pay Dispersion in the CEO's Top Team". *Strategic Management Journal*. 31(10): 1031–1053.

Goltz, J. (2013). "Not a Question of Fair Play". *The New York Times*. December 19, p. B10.

Gomez-Mejia, L. R. and D. B. Balkin (1992). *Compensation, Organizational Strategy, and Firm Performance*. South-Western Series in Human Resources Managemnent. South-Western Pub.

Gomez-Mejia, L. R. and T. M. Welbourne (1991). "Compensation Strategies in a Global Context". *Human Resource Planning*. 14(1): 29–41.

Gooderham, P. N., O. Nordhaug, and K. Ringdal (1999). "Institutional and Rational Determinants of Organizational Practices: Human Resource Management Practices in European Firms". *Administrative Science Quarterly*. 44(3): 507–531.

Gundolf, K. and M. Filser (2013). "Management Research and Religion: A Citation Analysis". *Journal of Business Ethics*. 112: 1240–1247.

Hastings, D. F. (1999). "Lincoln Electric's Harsh Lessons From International Expansion". *Harvard Business Review*. (May–June): 162–178.

Hilary, G. and K. W. Hui (2009). "Does Religion Matter in Corporate Decision Making in America?" *Journal of Financial Economics*. 93(3): 455–473.

Hofstede, G. (1980). *Culture's Consequences: International Differences in Work-Related Values*. Beverly Hills, CA: Sage Publications.

Hofstede, G. (1991). *Cultures and Organizations. Software of the Mind*. London: McGraw-Hill.

Hofstede, G. (2001). *Culture's Consequences: Comparing Values, Behaviors, Institutions, and Organizations Across Nations*. Thousand Oaks: Sage Publications.

Hofstede, G. and M. H. Bond (1988). "The Confucius Connection: From Cultural Roots to Economic Growth". *Organizational Dynamics*. 16(4): 4–21.

Hohenberg, S. and C. Homburg (2016). "Motivating Sales Reps for Innovation Selling in Different Cultures". *Journal of Marketing*. 80(March): 101–120.

Holmstrom, B. and P. Milgrom (1991). "Multitask Principal-Agent Analyses: Incentive Contracts, Asset Ownership, and Job Design". *Journal of Law, Economics, and Organization*. 7(0): 24–52.

Homburg, C., O. Jensen, and H. Krohmer (2008). "Configurations of Marketing and Sales: A Taxonomy". *Journal of Marketing*. 72(2): 133–154.

Hui, C. H. and H. G. Triandis (1986). "Individualism-Collectivism: A Study of Cross-Cultural Researchers". *Journal of Cross-Cultural Psychology*. 17(2): 225–248.

Jencks, C. and S. E. Mayer (1990). "The Social Consequences of Growing Up in a Poor Neighborhood". In: *Inner-City Poverty in the United States*. Ed. by M. G. H. McGeary and L. E. Lynn. Washington, DC: National Academy of Sciences.

John, G. and B. Weitz (1989). "Salesforce Compensation: An Empirical Investigation of Factors Related to Use of Salary Versus Incentive Compensation". *Journal of Marketing Research*. 26(February): 1–14.

Jones, D. A. and M. L. Martens (2009). "The Mediating Role of Overall Fairness and the Moderating Role of Trust Certainty in Justice–Criteria Relationships: The Formation and Use of Fairness Heuristics In the Workplace". *Journal of Organizational Behavior.* 30(8): 1025–1051.

Joseph, K. and M. U. Kalwani (1995). "The Impact of Environmental. Uncertainty on the Design of Salesforce Compensation Plans". *Marketing Letters.* 6(3): 183–197.

Joseph, K. and M. Kalwani (1998). "The Role of Bonus Pay in Salesforce Compensation Plans". *Industrial Marketing Management.* 27(2): 147–159.

Joseph, K. and A. Thevaranjan (1998). "Monitoring and Incentives in Sales Organizations: An Agency-Theoretic Perspective". *Marketing Science.* 17(2): 107–123.

Keshavarz, A., D. Rouziès, F. Kramarz, B. Quelin, M. Segalla, and M. Ahearne (2017). "How Do Firms Value Sales Career Paths?" working paper.

Kim, M. C. and L. M. McAlister (2011). "Stock Market Reaction to Unexpected Growth in Marketing Expenditure: Negative for Salesforce, Contingent on Spending Level for Advertising". *Journal of Marketing.* 75(3): 68–85.

Krafft, M., S. Albers, and R. Lal (2004). "Relative Explanatory Power of Agency Theory and Transaction Cost Analysis in German Salesforces". *International Journal of Research in Marketing.* 21: 265–283.

Lal, R. and V. Srinivasan (1993). "Compensation Plans for Single and Multi-Product Salesforces: An Application of the Holmstrom-Milgrom Model". *Management Science.* 39: 777–793.

Lal, R., D. Outland, and R. Staelin (1994). "Salesforce Compensation Plans: An Individual-Level Analysis". *Marketing Letters.* 2: 117–130.

Larkin, I., L. Pierce, and F. Gino (2012). "The Psychological Costs of Pay-For-Performance: Implications for the Strategic Compensation of Employees". *Strategic Management Journal.* 33(10): 1194–1214.

Lechner, C. M., R. K. Silbereisen, M. J. Tomasik, and J. Wasilewski (2015). "Getting Going and Letting Go: Religiosity Fosters Opportunity-Congruent Coping with Work-Related Uncertainties". *Journal of Psychology.* 50(3): 205–214.

Lerner, M. (1980). *The Belief in a Just World: A Fundamental Delusion.* New York, NY: Plenum Press.

Liu, S. S. (1998). "Reward Perceptions of Hong Kong and Mainland Chinese Sales Personnel". 18(3): 47–55.

Lo, D., M. Ghosh, and F. Lafontaine (2011). "The Incentive and Selection Roles of Sales Force Compensation Contracts". *Journal of Marketing Research.* 48(4): 781–798.

Miao, C. F., K. R. Evans, and P. Li (2017). "Effects of Top-Performer Rewards on Fellow Salespeople: A Double-Edged Sword". *Journal of Personal Selling & Sales Management.* 37(4): 280–297.

Midgley, D. (2013). "Strategic Marketing for the C-Suite: A Review of the Research Literature and Its Relevance to Senior Executives". *Foundations and Trends in Marketing.* 8(3–4): 147–341.

Miller, A. S. and J. P. Hoffman (1995). "Risk and Religion: An Explanation of Gender Differences in Religiosity". *Journal of the Scientific Study of Religion.* 34(1): 63–75.

Miller, J. S., P. W. Hom, and L. R. Gomez-Mejia (2001). "The High Cost of Low Wages: Does Maquiladora Compensation Reduce Turnover?" *Journal of International Business Studies.* 32(3): 585–595.

Misra, S., A. Coughlan, and C. Narasimhan (2005). "Salesforce Compensation: An Analytical and Empirical Examination of the Agency Theoretic Approach". *Quantitative Marketing and Economics.* 3(1): 5–39.

Misra, S. and H. S. Nair (2011). "A Structural Model of Sales-Force Compensation Dynamics: Estimation and Field Implementation". *Quantitative Marketing and Economics.* 9(3): 211–225.

Money, B. R. and J. L. Graham (1999). "Salesperson Performance, Pay, and Job Satisfaction: Tests of a Model Using Data Collected in the United States and Japan". *Journal of International Business Studies.* 30(1): 149–172.

Mowen, J. C. and M. M. Mowen (1991). "Time and Outcome Valuation: Implications for Marketing Decision Making". *Journal of Marketing.* 55(October): 55–62.

Murphy William, H. and N. Li (2012). "A Multi-Nation Study of Sales Manager Effectiveness with Global Implications". *Industrial Marketing Management.* 41: 1152–1163.

Nickerson, J. A. and T. R. Zenger (2008). "Envy, Comparison Costs, and the Economic Theory of the Firm". *Strategic Management Journal.* 29(13): 1429–1449.

Obloj, T. and M. Sengul (2012). "Incentive Life-cycles: Learning and the Division of Value in Firms". *Administrative Science Quarterly.* 57(2): 305–347.

O'Connell, K. and M. Blessington (2018). "Should Sales Compensation be Tested?" *The Marketing Journal.* January 29. URL: http://www.marketingjournal.org/should-sales-compensation%E2%80%A8-be-tested-kevin-oconnell-and-mark-blessington/ (accessed on 06/26/2018).

Oliver, R. L. and E. Anderson (1994). "An Empirical Test of the Consequences of Behavior- and Outcome-Based Sales Control Systems". *Journal of Marketing.* 58: 53–67.

Onyemah, V., D. Iacobucci, and D. Rouziès (2018). "The Impact of Religiosity and Culture on Salesperson Job Satisfaction and Performance". *International Journal of Cross Cultural Management.* 18(2): 191–219.

Panagopoulos, N. G., N. Lee, E. B. Pullins, G. J. Avlonitis, P. Brassier, P. Guenzi, A. Humenberger, P. Kwiatek, T. W. Loe, E. Oksanen-Ylikoski, R. M. Peterson, B. Rogers, and D. C. Weilbaker (2011). "Internationalizing Sales Research: Current Status, Opportunities and Challenges". *Journal of Personal Selling & Sales Management.* 31(3): 219–242.

Piercy, N. F., G. S. Low, and D. W. Cravens (2011). "Country Differences Concerning Sales Organizations and Salesperson Antecedents of Unit Effectiveness". *Journal of World Business.* 46: 104–115.

Piketty, T. (2014). *Capital in the Twenty-First Century.* Cambridge, MA: Harvard University Press.

Plender, J. (2012). "The Code That Forms A Bar To Harmony: Capitalism In Crisis". *Financial Times*. January 9, p. 5.

Proskauer-International HR Best Practices (2010). www:proskauer.com, page 1.

Ramaswami, S. N. and J. Singh (2003). "Antecedents and Consequences of Merit Pay Fairness for Industrial Salespeople". *Journal of Marketing*. 67: 46–66.

Ronen, S. and O. Shenkar (2013). "Mapping World Cultures: Cluster Formation, Sources and Implications". *Journal of International Business Studies*. 44(9): 867–897.

Rouziès, D. (1992). "The Effects of a Salesperson's Utilities on Optimal Sales Force Compensation Structures". Doctoral Dissertation, McGill University.

Rouziès, D., A. Coughlan, E. Anderson, and D. Iacobucci (2009). "Determinants of Pay Levels and Structures in Sales Organizations". *Journal of Marketing*. 73(November): 92–104.

Rouziès, D. and J. Hulland (2014). "Does Marketing and Sales Integration Always Pay Off? Evidence from a Social Capital Perspective". *Journal of the Academy of Marketing Science*. 42(5): 511–527. September.

Rouziès, D., V. Onyemah, and D. Iacobucci (2017). "A Multi-Cultural Study of Salespeople's Behavior in Individual Pay-For-Performance Compensation Systems: When Managers Are More Equal and Less Fair Than Others". *Journal of Personal Selling & Sales Management*. 37(3): 198–212.

Rouziou, M., R. Dugan, D. Rouziès, and D. Iacobucci (2018a). "Brand Assets and Pay Fairness As Two Routes to Enhancing Social Capital in Sales Organizations". *Journal of Personal Selling & Sales Management*. DOI: 10.1080/08853134.2017.1384699.

Rouziou, M., D. Rouziès, and D. Iacobucci (2018b). "Salespeople's Pay Comparisons: The Differential Effect of Comparison Foci on Sales Performance". Working paper.

Saroglou, V. and A. B. Cohen (2011). "Psychology of Culture and Religion: Introduction to the *JCCP* Special Issue". *Journal of Cross-Cultural Psychology*. 42(8): 1309–1319.

Schuler, R. S. and N. Rogovsky (1998). "Understanding Compensation Practice Variations Across Firms: The Impact of National Culture". *Journal of International Business Studies.* 29(1): 159–177.

Schwartz, S. H. (1999). "A Theory of Cultural Values and Some Implications for Work". *Applied Psychology.* 48(1): 23–47.

Segalla, M., D. Rouziès, M. Besson, and B. A. Weitz (2006). "A Cross-National Investigation of Incentive Sales Compensation". *International Journal of Research in Marketing.* 23: 419–433.

Steenburgh, T. (2008). "Effort or Timing: The Effect of Lump-Sum Bonuses". *Quantitative Marketing & Economics.* 6(3): 235–256.

Sung, S. Y., J. N. Choi, and S.-C. Kang (2017). "Incentive Pay and Firm Performance: Moderating Roles of Procedural Justice Climate and Environmental Turbulence". *Human Resource Management.* 56(2): 287–305.

The Economist (2011). "The Art of Selling". 10–22, 77.

Tosi, H. L. and T. Greckhamer (2004). "Culture and CEO Compensation". *Organization Science.* 15(6): 657–670.

U.S. Bureau of Labor Statistics (2015). "Labor Force Statistics for the Current Population Survey". URL: http://wwww.bls.gov/cps/cpsaat 11.htm (accessed on 11/28/2016).

Vroom, V. H. (1964). *Work and Motivation.* New York: Wiley.

Walker Jr., O. C., G. A. Churchill Jr., and N. M. Ford (1977). "Motivation and Performance in Industrial Selling : Present Knowledge and Needed Research". *Journal of Marketing Research.* 14: 156–168.

Weber, E. U. and C. Hsee (1998). "Cross-Cultural Differences in Risk Perception, But Cross-Cultural Similarities in Attitudes Towards Perceived Risk". *Management Science.* 44: 1205–1217.

Weber, L. (2015). "Careers: Bright Future in Sales? Millennials Are Hesitant". *The Wall Street Journal.* February 4.

Werner, S. and S. G. Ward (2004). "Recent Compensation Research: An Eclectic Review". *Human Resource Management Review.* 14(2): 201–227.

Wheeler, L. (1966). "Motivation As a Determinant of Upward Comparison". *Journal of Experimental Social Psychology.* 1: 27–31.

Wheeler, L., K. G. Shaver, R. A. Jones, G. R. Goethals, J. Cooper, J. E. Robinson, C. L. Gruder, and K. W. Butzine (1969). "Factors Determining Choice of a Comparison Other". *Journal of Experimental Social Psychology*. 5: 219–232.

Williamson, O. E. (1981). "The Economics of Organization: The Transaction Cost Approach". *American Journal of Sociology*. 87(3): 548–577.

Zimmerman, D. J. (2003). "Peer Effects in Academic Outcomes: Evidence From a Natural Experiment". *Review of Economics and Statistics*. 85(1): 9–23.

Zoltners, A. A., P. K. Sinha, and S. E. Lorimer (2006). *How to Design and Implement Plans That Work: The Complete Guide to Sales Force Incentive Compensation*. AMACOM.

Zoltners, A. A., P. K. Sinha, and S. E. Lorimer (2009). *Building a Winning Sales Force: Powerful Strategies for Driving High Performance*. AMACOM.

Zoltners, A. A., P. K. Sinha, and S. E. Lorimer (2015). "There Is No One System for Paying Your Global Sales Force". *Harvard Business Review*. November 13.